The God of
the Way
Study Series
• • •

The GOD of the OTHER SIDE

BIBLE STUDY GUIDE | SIX SESSIONS

Kathie Lee Gifford
with Joanne Moody

Harper*Christian*
Resources

The God of the Other Side
© 2024 by Kathie Lee Gifford

Published in Grand Rapids, Michigan, by HarperChristian Resources. HarperChristian Resources is a registered trademark of Harper-Collins Christian Publishing, Inc.

Requests for information should be sent to customercare@harpercollins.com.

ISBN 978-0-310-15693-2 (softcover)
ISBN 978-0-310-15694-9 (ebook)

First Printing December 2023 / Printed in the United States of America

Contents

A Note from Kathie Lee

The genesis for the oratorio *The God of the Way* began several years ago when I was on a rabbinical study trip to Israel led by an extraordinary teacher named Rod Van-Solkema and his lovable and gifted wife, Libby. I appreciated being shepherded by a married couple, and I loved watching them synchronize their strengths in a way that completely complemented their power as a couple. They both have sharp minds and tender hearts—an irresistible combination!

On one particular day, Rod began by telling us the story from Matthew's Gospel in which Jesus told his disciples to get into their boat and meet him on the other side of the lake, just before he came walking to them on the water. As Matthew writes, "Immediately Jesus made the disciples get into the boat and go on ahead of him to *the other side*, while he dismissed the crowd" (14:22, emphasis added). I was familiar with the story—I had been traveling to the Holy Land to take part in intense rabbinical study trips ever since I was a teenager. I was always hoping to learn more truth about the Scriptures and gain an even deeper understanding of what the Word of God said in its original Hebrew and Greek texts.

I had always assumed that when Jesus sent the disciples to "the other side," it simply referred to the other side of the Sea of Galilee. But the fascinating part of studying rabbinically is that you also learn context, including customs of the culture when Jesus lived on the earth as well as the geopolitical realities of ancient times. Rod taught us that "the other side" actually meant something very different from and more profound than just a physical location. When he did this, the story took on much deeper meaning for me.

Rod explained that the area Jesus was telling his disciples to meet him was the Decapolis—ten ancient villages where the original Canaanites had fled from Joshua's invading army of Hebrews after they had crossed over the Jordan River to conquer the Holy Land. These villages were inhabited by people who worshiped many gods and idols. They sacrificed babies to the gods Moloch and Chemosh and others and participated in all manner of sexual perversion. They were the opposite of a devout Jew and were considered unclean.

We can only imagine how the twelve disciples reacted when they heard that Jesus basically was telling them to go to the ancient-day equivalent of Sin City!

What would we do today if Jesus asked us to do the same? Would we be as confused and terrified as the disciples were 2,000 years ago? Would we decide to say, "No, Jesus. I mean, you're cool and you do amazing miracles and I like all your stories, but what you're asking defies everything I have ever been taught. I'll catch up with you when you get back and hear all about it"? Or would we trust that he had a purpose for everything he said and did, and maybe that if we followed him, he would lead us on the adventure of a lifetime?

The God of the Other Side is still calling out to his followers to step out of their comfort zones and follow where he leads—regardless of where that might take us. The question for each of us today is whether we are willing to heed his voice. Are we willing, just like the twelve disciples of Jesus, to obey his call and get into the boat?

How to Use This Guide

The Lord once said to a Hebrew prophet, "As a shepherd looks after his scattered flock when he is with them, so will I look after my sheep. I will rescue them from all the places where they were scattered on a day of clouds and darkness" (Ezekiel 34:12). The prophet's words reveal that God is not content to just let people abide in darkness. Instead, he pursues them like a shepherd pursues a lost sheep, seeking them until they are found.

It is no coincidence that Jesus, in the New Testament, often referred to himself as a "good shepherd" (John 10:11). His mission was "to seek and to save the lost" (Luke 19:10). This often led to him sharing meals with those whom the religious leaders of the day deemed to be on the outside—those with whom "proper" Jews did not associate. They complained, "This man welcomes sinners and eats with them" (Luke 15:2). Jesus, in response, told a parable about a shepherd who loses a sheep. He asked these leaders, "Doesn't he leave the ninety-nine in the open country and go after the lost sheep until he finds it?" (verse 4).

In this study, we will look at the stories of several individuals in the Bible whom Jesus went to "the other side" to reach. Before you begin, note that there are a few ways you can go through this material. You can experience this study with others in a group (such as a Bible study, Sunday school class, or any other small-group gathering), or you may choose to go through the content on your own. Either way, know that the videos for each session are available for you to view at any time by following the instructions provided on the inside cover of this study guide.

Group Study

Each of the sessions is divided into two parts: (1) a group study section and (2) a personal study section. The group study section is intended to provide a basic framework on how to open your time together, get the most out of the video content, and discuss the key ideas together that were presented in the teaching. Each session includes the following:

- **Welcome:** A short note about the topic of the session for you to read on your own before you meet together as a group.

- **Connect:** A few icebreaker questions to get you and your group members thinking about the topic and interacting with each other.
- **Watch:** An outline of the key points that will be covered in each video teaching to help you follow along, stay engaged, and take notes.
- **Discuss:** Questions to help your group reflect on the material presented and apply it to your lives. In each session, you will be given four "suggested" questions and four "additional" questions to use as time allows.
- **Respond:** A short personal exercise to help reinforce the key ideas.
- **Pray:** A place for you to record prayer requests and praises for the week.

If you are doing this study in a group, make sure you have your own copy of this study guide so you can write down your thoughts, responses, and reflections and have access to the videos via streaming. You will also want to have a copy of the *God of the Way* book, as reading it alongside the curriculum will provide you with deeper insights. (See the notes at the beginning of each group session and personal study section on which chapters of the book you should read before the next group session.) Finally, keep these points in mind:

- **Facilitation:** If you are doing this study in a group, you will want to appoint someone to serve as a facilitator. This person will be responsible for starting the video and keeping track of time during discussions and activities. If *you* have been chosen for this role, there are some resources in the back of this guide that can help you lead your group through the study.

- **Faithfulness:** Your small group is a place where tremendous growth can happen as you reflect on the Bible, ask questions, and learn what God is doing in other people's lives. For this reason, be fully committed and attend each session so you can build trust and rapport with the other members.

- **Friendship:** The goal of any small group is to serve as a place where people can share, learn about God, and build friendships. So seek to make your group a "safe place." Be honest about your thoughts and feelings . . . but also listen carefully to everyone else's thoughts, feelings, and opinions. Keep anything personal that your group members share in confidence so that you can create a community where people can heal, be challenged, and grow spiritually.

If you are going through this study on your own, read the opening Welcome section and reflect on the questions in the Connect section. Watch the video and use the prompts provided to take notes. Finally, personalize the questions and exercises in the Discuss and Respond sections. Close by recording any requests you want to pray about during the week.

Personal Study

As the name implies, the personal study is for you to work through on your own during the week. Each exercise is designed to help you explore the key ideas you uncovered during your group time and delve into passages of Scripture that will help you apply those principles to your life. Go at your own pace, doing a little each day or all at once, and spend a few moments in silence to listen to what God might be saying to you. Each personal study will include:

- **Opening:** A brief introduction to lead you into the personal study for the day.
- **Scripture:** A few passages on the topic of the day for you to read and review.
- **Reflection:** Questions for you to answer related to the passages you just read.
- **Prayer:** A prompt to help you express what you've studied in a prayer to God.

If you are doing this study as part of a group, and you are unable to finish (or even start) these personal studies for the week, you should still attend the group time. Be assured that you are still wanted and welcome even if you don't have your "homework" done. The group studies and personal studies are intended to help you hear what God wants you to hear and learn how to apply what he is saying to your life. So, as you go through this study, be listening for him to speak to you as you learn about what it means to follow the *God of the Other Side*.

WEEK 1

BEFORE GROUP MEETING	Read Part 4 and chapter 13 in *The God of the Way* Read the Welcome section (page 3)
GROUP MEETING	Discuss the Connect questions Watch the video teaching for session 1 Discuss the questions that follow as a group Do the closing exercise and pray (pages 3–14)
PERSONAL STUDY – DAY 1	Complete the daily study (pages 16–17)
PERSONAL STUDY – DAY 2	Complete the daily study (pages 18–19)
PERSONAL STUDY – DAY 3	Complete the daily study (pages 20–21)
PERSONAL STUDY – DAY 4	Complete the daily study (pages 22–23)
PERSONAL STUDY – DAY 5 (before week 2 group meeting)	Complete the daily study (pages 24–25) Read chapter 14 in *The God of the Way* Complete any unfinished personal studies

The Other Side

GOD NEVER PASSES US BY

*Immediately Jesus made the disciples get into the boat
and go on ahead of him to the other side, while he dismissed the
crowd. After he had dismissed them, he went up on a mountainside
by himself to pray. Later that night, he was there alone, and the
boat was already a considerable distance from land, buffeted
by the waves because the wind was against it.*

MATTHEW 14:22–24

Welcome | Read On Your Own

Welcome to *The God of the Other Side*. Over the course of the next few weeks, you and your group will look at the stories in the Bible of the Demoniac, the Samaritan Woman, the Prodigal Son, Cornelius and Peter, and the four men who brought their paralyzed friend to Jesus—all with the goal of exploring why they are so important to us today. But before we embark on that journey, we first need to look at what the "other side" meant in the culture of Jesus' day.

In the Gospels, we often read stories of Jesus sending his disciples to the other side of the Sea of Galilee. This was an area on the eastern shore known as the Decapolis (Greek for "ten cities"). The people of the region served the gods of the Greeks and the Romans, and thus the territory was considered off-limits for the Jewish people, as even stepping foot there could make them ceremonially unclean. But not so for Jesus. He was willing to go to anyplace where the lost could be found . . . and bring his disciples along for the ride.

The God of the Other Side continues to call his disciples to do this today. But just like the twelve, we do not like what the other side represents. The other side is unknown. It is out of our comfort zone. It is the last place on earth we would ever want to be. We would prefer God call us to minister to those in need in places that are safe—places that do not require us to exert much faith in him. But the God of the Other Side will not allow us to settle for the safe and familiar! He wants to reveal himself to us in his full glory by taking us to the other side.

When he does, we have the assurance that he will be with us every step of the way. Just as Jesus was with the disciples, he will be with us today. We only need to heed his calling.

Connect | 15 minutes

If any of your group members don't know each other, take a few minutes to introduce yourselves. Then, to get things started, discuss one of the following questions:

- How would you describe your primary goal or hope for participating in this study? (In other words, why are you here?)

  — *or* —

- What are some of the places that the "other side" represents in your life?

Watch | 20 minutes

Now it's time to watch the video for this session, which you can access by playing the DVD or through streaming (see the instructions provided on the inside front cover). As you watch, use the following outline to record any thoughts or concepts that stand out to you.

I. What was the "other side" of the Sea of Galilee in Jesus' day?

  A. Jesus sent his disciples across the Sea of Galilee after the miracle of feeding the 5,000. Meanwhile, he went up a mountainside to pray (see Matthew 14:13–23).

   1. We read this and think it was no big deal—after all, the Sea of Galilee is not a big lake and it wasn't a lengthy crossing. But the disciples would have thought the exact opposite.

   2. The "other side" of the Sea of Galilee was a place that was forbidden to Jews. Jesus was telling his disciples to go to a location they had been told their entire lives *not* to go.

   3. The disciples would have recognized that if they went to that place and got out of the boat, they would have been considered ceremonially unclean according to Jewish law.

  B. We can imagine that in this moment, given the events of the day, there would have been many conflicting thoughts and emotions welling up within the disciples.

   1. Remember that the disciples had just witnessed an extraordinary miracle in which Jesus fed more than 5,000 people with two fish and five loaves, with twelve huge basketfuls left over.

   2. The disciples had seen Jesus bring abundant provision out of nothing. They would naturally have wanted to talk about this miracle and celebrate it.

The Decapolis

The *Decapolis* is a name given in the Bible (and by ancient writers) to a region located east and southeast of the Sea of Galilee. It was given this name because the area consisted of ten cities within its borders (Greek *deca* meaning "ten" and *polis* meaning "city"). While the names of these cities vary among the ancient writers, Pliny the Elder refers to them as Scythopolis, Philadelphia, Raphanae, Gadara, Hippos, Dios, Pella, Gerasa, Canatha, and Damascus.[1]

All of these cities except Scythopolis, the capital, were located east of the Jordan River in the territory that had been given to the tribe of Manasseh during the time of Moses (see Joshua 13:29–31). When the people of Manasseh failed to drive the Canaanites out of their land, they pressed the people that remained into slavery (see Judges 1:27–28). The territory was later captured by Alexander the Great around 330 BC. He had a dream of "Hellenizing" (making Greek) the entire world. This ideal was taken up by others after his death.

The ten cities appear to have been founded by the Greek settler-soldiers of the Seleucid and Ptolemaic kingdoms that followed after Alexander's empire. Then, in 64–63 BC, Pompey the Great brought the entire region under the control of Rome. He incorporated all ten Greek cities into a league known as the Decapolis. The residents of these cities appear to have welcomed Roman rule, as it finally gave them religious autonomy from the neighboring Jewish regions. Rome even provided support for some of their cultural practices and religious rites.[2]

The Decapolis is mentioned three times in the New Testament. In Matthew 4:25, we read that "large crowds from Galilee, the Decapolis, Jerusalem, Judea and the region across the Jordan followed [Jesus]." In Mark 7:31, "Jesus left the vicinity of Tyre and went through Sidon, down to the Sea of Galilee and into the region of the Decapolis." In Mark 5:20, the former demon-possessed man "went away and began to tell in the Decapolis how much Jesus had done for him." Mark places the actual location where Jesus landed as "the region of the Gerasenes" (verse 1), most likely referring to the town of Gadara located thirteen miles south.

3. But instead, Jesus told them to get into a boat and cross to the other side of the lake. He was basically casting them into the abyss. But he was also about to change their lives!

C. The disciples were not just rowing across the lake on a ministry trip—and we have to consider the fact that they would not have wanted to get into that boat in the first place.

1. The Jewish people traditionally believed that only bad things happened on the water. Even some of the fishermen in that day could not swim. They only went out a little ways to fish.

2. The fishing boats of that day were also small. The twelve disciples would have crowded into the boat to fit. Given all this, they would have been terrified at the idea of the crossing.

3. The disciples embarked on this epic adventure and had no idea—in their terror, anger, disappointment, and (mostly) confusion—what they were about to witness.

II. What happened when a storm suddenly rose up as the disciples crossed the lake?

A. The disciples were well across the lake when a furious storm came up that caused the waves to buffet the boat (see Matthew 14:24). Their greatest fears were being realized.

1. The Jewish people believed that chaos and calamity lived under the water. In the midst of all the mayhem on the Sea of Galilee, the disciples would have wondered why Jesus had abandoned them.

2. We all wonder the same when we encounter calamity in our lives. Fear causes us to think that God has abandoned us. We start to act as if nobody cares about us.

3. However, we have to remember that God's perfect love drives out fear (see 1 John 4:18). We have a heavenly Father who does not abandon us but comes to our rescue.

B. As the disciples struggled to keep the boat afloat, they saw a figure striding across the waves. They thought they were seeing a ghost (see Matthew 14:25–26).

1. At first they were terrified of this "creature" coming toward them, but then they realized it was Jesus. This caused even more confusion—was this person really him?

2. It was at this point that Peter blurted out what was on his mind. He asked Jesus—if it was truly him—to call him to step out of the boat onto the waves (see verse 28).

3. Peter wanted to hear the voice of his Good Shepherd in that moment. As Jesus had said, "My sheep listen to my voice; I know them, and they follow me" (John 10:27).

C. Jesus invited Peter to come, so the disciple stepped out of the boat and began to walk on the water (see Matthew 14:29). In doing so, Peter was taking a profound step of faith.

1. Peter's action is a great metaphor for our lives. We all would rather remain in the boat with the others where we feel it is safe, but Jesus calls us to step out in faith.

2. All was going well for Peter until he took his eyes off Jesus (see verse 30). The same is true for us when we take a step of faith. We have to stay focused on Jesus.

3. Jesus caught Peter—just as he catches us when we doubt—and lifted him up. When they climbed back into the boat, the wind suddenly died down (see verses 31–32).

III. What is the significance of Jesus walking across the surface of the water?

A. There are several passages in the Old Testament where God says that he treads on the water:

1. "He alone stretches out the heavens and treads on the waves of the sea" (Job 9:8).

2. "This is what the LORD says—he who made a way through the sea, a path through the mighty waters" (Isaiah 43:16).

3. "Your path led through the sea, your way through the mighty waters, though your footprints were not seen" (Psalm 77:19).

B. The miracle of Jesus walking on the water recalls several miracles from the Old Testament and indicates how the Messiah came to bring God's *shalom* to the chaos.

1. Elijah and Elisha split the Jordan River and crossed through it (see 2 Kings 2:8, 14). God also used Moses to split the Rea Sea for the Israelites (see Exodus 14:21–22).

The Hebrew Word *Shalom*

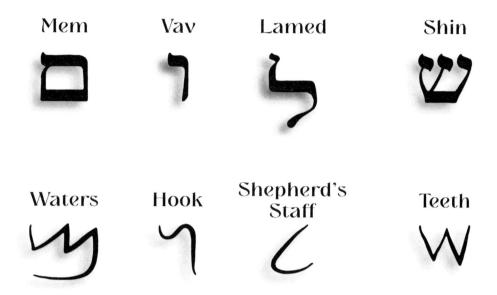

Mem   Vav   Lamed   Shin

Waters   Hook   Shepherd's Staff   Teeth

Like other ancient writing systems, the Hebrew alphabet was originally written using a pictographic script. Over time, these pictograms evolved into a Hebrew script. However, Hebrew is still a pictorial language in that its letters can represent certain symbols and images. The Hebrew word *shalom*, depicted above, is comprised of four such symbols: (1) teeth, (2) a shepherd's staff, (3) a hook, and (4) a storm. When put together—and remember that Hebrew is read right to left—the word *shalom* means: "God destroyed (teeth) with his authority (shepherd's staff) the hook (literal hook) of chaos and calamity (storm) in our lives."

2. In the creation account, we read that God's spirit moved over the waters, which represent chaos (see Genesis 1:2). God thus brought his *shalom* to the chaos. In the same way, Jesus strode over the surface of the stormy water of the Sea of Galilee and brought his *shalom*.

3. Hebrew is a pictorial language. The four pictorial symbols that define *shalom* are teeth, a shepherd's rod, a hook, and a storm (a tsunami). God destroyed (teeth), with his authority (rod), the grasp (hook) of chaos and calamity (storm) in our lives.

IV. What importance does this story of Jesus walking on the water hold for us today?

A. Jesus calls us into an intimate relationship with himself where we trust in him completely and then step out in faith so we can witness his glory.

1. When we look at this story, it is hard to fault the eleven disciples who decided to stay in the boat. If we are honest, most of us would have done the same.

2. But Peter had such intimacy with Jesus that he knew he could trust his master's voice. He had "unction" in the sense that his deep belief in Jesus led him to take action.

3. Jesus compelled the disciples to travel to the other side of the Sea of Galilee—and compelled Peter to step out of the boat—so he could reveal his glory to them.

B. Sometimes, there are moments in our lives where the enemy causes chaos and calamity to arise in our lives, just as the tumultuous storm suddenly arose in this story.

    1. The enemy likes to intimidate us with the "wind and the waves" that surround us.

    2. But it is in these instances that we need to pay attention. When intimidation and calamity enter our lives, it usually indicates that a "promotion" is about to happen.

    3. The Lord is about to do something miraculous in our lives that reveals his glory. Just like the disciples, we will see Jesus walking to us across the surface of the chaos.

C. The point of this story for us today is that we are going to the "other side" every day with Jesus.

    1. There are going to be obstacles, storms, and intimidations that scream out to us, "Don't move! You will only be safe if you remain where you are in the boat."

    2. Jesus says to us, "Come walk on the water in the midst of the chaos." He invites us to follow after him—and when we obey, we will see him do miraculous things in our lives.

    3. There are many of us today waiting for Jesus to reach out, grasp us by the hand, and lift us out of the waves. We can trust he has the power and willingness to rescue us.

Discuss | 35 minutes

Take some time to discuss what you just watched by answering the following questions. There are some suggested questions below to help you begin your discussion, but feel free to pick any of the additional questions as time allows.

Suggested Questions

1. Ask someone to read aloud the story of Jesus walking on the water in Matthew 14:22–33. Notice that Jesus went up a mountainside by himself to pray and sent the disciples on ahead of him—all the while knowing that a storm was brewing on the lake. Why do you think he did this? How do you think the disciples felt about this?

2. The "other side" of the Sea of Galilee was the location of the Decapolis—a place forbidden to the Jews where the people practiced pagan religions. So why did Jesus instruct the disciples to go there? What do you think he was revealing to them about the lengths the God of the Other Side will go to reach lost and hurting people?

3. Ask someone to read Job 9:8, Isaiah 43:16, and Psalm 77:19. How do these passages from the Old Testament prophesy what Jesus was going to do on the water that night? Considering how the Jewish people felt about water, what would it mean for the disciples to have witnessed Jesus walking on the water and calming the storm?

4. The diagram on page 9 represents the Hebrew word *shalom*. It is comprised of four symbols: teeth, a shepherd's rod, a hook, and a storm. What is the significance of each image? What does this tell you about Jesus' role in calming the chaos in our lives?

Additional Questions

5. Take a moment to read aloud Matthew 14:13–21. How do you think this miracle prepared the disciples to obey Jesus' call to go to the other side of the Sea of Galilee? How would witnessing Jesus' power in such a profound way bolster their faith?

6. It is easy to fault Peter for taking his eyes off Jesus in the midst of the storm, but we have to remember that he was the *only* disciple who was even willing to get out of the boat. What enabled him to take that step of faith? What does this say about the importance of having a strong relationship with Jesus if we want to likewise witness his power in our lives?

7. Ask someone to read aloud Genesis 1:1–2. Notice in this passage the Holy Spirit was "hovering over the waters" of the "formless and empty" earth. What does this tell us about how the Lord interacts with the chaos and calamity in our lives?

8. Jesus calls us to go to the "other side" with him each and every day of our lives. When is a recent time that he called you to step out of your comfort zone and do something you would not normally have done? What happened as a result of your obedience?

Respond | 10 minutes

Review the outline for the video teaching and any notes you took. In the space below, write down your most significant takeaway from this session.

Pray | 10 minutes

Praying for one another is one of the most important things you can do as a community. So use this time wisely and make it more than just a "closing prayer" to end your group experience. Be intentional about sharing your prayers, reviewing how God is answering your prayers, and actually praying for one another as a group. Use the space below to write down any requests so that you and your group members can continue to pray about them in the week ahead.

Name   Request

Personal Study

You are on a journey toward a better understanding of the God of the Other Side. A key part of that growth, regardless of where you are spiritually, involves studying Scripture. This is the goal of these personal studies—to help you explore what the Bible has to say and how to apply the Word of God to your life. As you work through each of these exercises, be sure to write down your responses to the questions, as you will be given a few minutes to share your insights at the start of the next session if you are doing this study with others. If you are reading *The God of the Way* alongside this study, first read Part 4 and chapter 13 in the book.

-Day 1-

Called to the Other Side

As discussed in this week's group time, the "other side" represents those places in your life where you would rather not go—those places that make you feel fearful, anxious, and unsure about the future. What defines the other side will be different for every person. Your other side will not be the same as your neighbor's other side. What will take you out of your comfort zone won't necessarily be the same kinds of things that will take your friend out of his or her comfort zone. We all have different limits, expectations, histories, and giftings that directly impact how we respond—and our willingness to obey—our Savior's call to go to the other side.

In the story told in Matthew 14:22–36, the disciples were clear as to what the other side of the Sea of Galilee represented. As Jews, the Decapolis—where Jesus was telling them to go—was the absolute worst calling they could have received. The Decapolis was inhabited by pagans who committed every sin against the law from idol worship to child sacrifice.[3] To go there was a religious and social death sentence. The disciples would be deemed unclean.

While our "other sides" will vary, the trepidation we feel when facing them will be just the same as the disciples were feeling that night. We will ask the same questions that they were likely asking each other. *Does Jesus realize where he is sending us? What will happen when we get there? Is there anywhere else—seriously, anywhere else—where he can send us?*

The Bible is filled with stories of God's people being called to make the journey to the other side. Sometimes they willingly obeyed, but often they were just as afraid as the disciples when they received the call. This is how the Israelites felt during the Exodus when God called them to take a step of faith and trust that he would deliver them from an approaching army. The people could see no way forward. But God miraculously took them to the "other side."

Read | Exodus 14:10–22

Reflect

1. The Israelites thought they were free of the Egyptians. Pharaoh, the king of Egypt, had agreed to let them go after the Lord sent a series of ten plagues that devastated the country. But then Pharaoh thought twice about losing his Hebrew workforce and sent his army in pursuit. Now the Israelites were trapped . . . and terrified. How did Moses reassure the people that the Lord had not forgotten them?

2. God instructed Moses to raise his staff and stretch out his hand over the Red Sea. How did the Lord then provide a way for the people to get to the other side? What do you imagine they were thinking as they stepped out in faith to the Lord's command?

3. In the story of the disciples crossing the Sea of Galilee, the other side represented an unfamiliar place where they did not know what would happen in their future. How was this the same for the people of Israel as they crossed to the other side of the Red Sea?

4. The story of God parting the Red Sea is a literal example of God helping us get to the other side. How could this story apply to the other side that you are facing? Or, when is a time in the past that God "parted the sea" in a way that allowed you to get there?

Pray | End your time in prayer. Remember that the same God who parted the sea is the God who is guiding your steps today. You can trust in him wherever he leads.

— Day 2 —

Chaos in the Crossing

Have you ever been running late to an important event and, on your way, you hit every red light, got stuck behind every slow driver, and encountered every other delay possible? It can often seem that when you are the most desperate to arrive at your destination is when you will encounter the greatest number of obstacles on the way to getting there.

The same can seem true when God calls you to travel to whatever represents the "other side" in your life. You know where you are supposed to go, you obey God's calling (either courageously or with hesitation), and then—*bam!*—suddenly, it seems as if every obstacle possible is in your way. Your family opposes what you are doing. The paperwork gets held up. Self-doubt takes over. But, as noted in this week's teaching, it is when you encounter opposition that you need to watch for God to move, because a promotion is about to happen.

Facing challenges, obstacles, and setbacks in your calling is not a sign that you need to turn back. In fact, it means just the opposite. Whenever you confront chaos from the enemy, you need to press on and lean into Jesus even more, allowing him to bring you his perfect peace. This is what Jesus did to the wind and the waves on the stormy Sea of Galilee as the disciples pressed on to reach the other side. He will do it with your rough seas as well.

As you learned this week, the word *shalom* means more than peace. It represents God's authority over the chaos and calamity in this world. Intimidation and fear are not from the Lord. The enemy wants nothing more than to keep you from crossing to the other side—to prevent you from experiencing the power of God. Satan would like nothing more than for you to cave to the intimidation and doubt. You cannot let his tactics prevail! Instead, call them out for what they are—*lies*—and keep your focus on Jesus. Trust that whatever chaos and calamity have come into your life will be no match for the *shalom* that your Savior is offering to you.

Read | Matthew 8:23–27 and John 14:23–27

Reflect

1. In Matthew 8:23–27, we find Jesus on another boat with the disciples in another storm. How did Jesus calm this particular storm? How did the disciples respond to this miracle?

2. In John 14:23–27, Jesus told his disciples that he would not be with them on earth much longer, but that his presence would never leave them. What did Jesus say he would leave them? How does Jesus' peace differ from the peace the world offers?

3. When have you encountered obstacles in pursuing something that you felt God was calling you to do? (These could be emotional obstacles like fear and doubt or more tangible obstacles like logistics or others' opinions—anything that would get in the way of your calling.) How did you respond to those obstacles?

4. When have you experienced peace, or *shalom*, in the way these passages present it? Where do you need more of Jesus' *shalom* today?

Pray | Think about a storm that you are facing. Ask Jesus to meet you in that storm in the same way he met the disciples in their storm. Trust that he can calm the wind and the waves.

-Day 3-

Persevere in the Crossing

The first few days of a new adventure are always fresh and exciting. Maybe you've experienced this recently with moving to a new city, or starting a new job, or attending a new school. In the first few days, weeks, and months, you have boundless energy, adrenaline, and hope for the future. But then . . . the newness starts to wear off and the difficulties set in.

Not knowing your way around a new city is frustrating. Being the new kid at work is more troublesome than you thought. Not having a community of friends around you at your new school is disheartening. You have now forgotten whatever reasons you initially had for taking on this new adventure. Instead, you are wondering if you made a huge mistake.

When Jesus calls you to journey to the other side, it is rarely a quick trip. Rather, the crossing is more often long and arduous—and filled with obstacles and difficulties that at first you didn't foresee. A journey to the other side requires faith, obedience, and trust in the Lord, but it also requires a heavy dose of perseverance and steadfastness to see it through to the end. So, what do you do when your strength wavers? How do you keep on going?

Peter provides a prime example of not only how quickly we can lose faith in our calling but also what we should do when this happens to us. At first, Peter was filled with confidence and boldly began walking across the waves of the Sea of Galilee to Jesus. Yet it only took a few steps before the reality of the situation set in. Peter started to fear because of the wind and the waves. This caused him to doubt, which made him take his eyes off Jesus. When that happened, he started to sink.

But what Peter did next made all the difference: "When he saw the wind, he was afraid and, beginning to sink, cried out, 'Lord, save me!'" (Matthew 14:30). Peter cried out for help, and *immediately* Jesus rescued him. He will do the same in our lives. When we realize we have lost focus and need his strength to carry on, we need only call out to Jesus for help.

Read | 1 Kings 19:1–18

Reflect

1. Elijah had just experienced a great spiritual victory as the events of this passage unfold. He had prevailed over 450 false prophets of Baal and revealed Yahweh to be the one true God of Israel (see 1 Kings 18:16–46). But it didn't take long for him to lose hope in his mission. What happened that caused him to so quickly fall into despair?

2. Elijah was afraid and ran for his life. When he arrived in Beersheba, he sent his servant away and traveled a day's journey into a desolate wilderness. What did he do when he finally came to the end of his strength? What happened next in the story?

3. What did the Lord ultimately say to Elijah that convinced him to persevere?

4. It is easy to take our eyes off God and focus on fear, anxiety, and doubt. Where in your life have you taken your eyes off him? How could you refocus on him today?

Pray | Come before the Lord during your prayer time. Be honest with him about your fears and anxieties. Call out to him for help, knowing that he always hears the cries of his children.

−Day 4−

A Daily Call to the Other Side

When you picture going to the "other side," you may envision this type of calling as being reserved for just the biggest and most important moments in life. You know the ones—that mission trip to a faraway place that occurs once a year, or that service day when everyone in the church commits to assisting the community, or that time near the end of the year when you and your family sacrificially give an extra amount to help another family in need.

But the reality is that the Savior calls you to go to the other side every single day. When Jesus was on earth, he was continually reaching out to those whom society deemed to be on the "other side" and too far gone to save. He was always ministering among the sick and the poor and those whom the culture of the day had shunned. In each of these excursions, he was accompanied by the twelve disciples, who took part in every act of his ministry.

As we have discussed, the other side can be *anything* that represents the unknown and uncertain to you. In some cases, just stepping out of your comfort zone to talk with another person who you sense needs your help can be a trip to the other side. Jesus once told a parable about this in which the people who were serving him didn't even realize they were doing so because their actions were so . . . ordinary. They thought they were just providing food, water, clothing, and shelter to those in need. But God said, "Whatever you did for one of the least of these brothers and sisters of mine, you did for me" (Matthew 25:40).

The Lord once told his people to not "despise the day of small things" (Zechariah 4:10). Even the seemingly mundane moments of life can have eternal significance. Our part is not to judge whether what we are doing is "great enough" to have merit. Our role is not to weigh whether we feel we are equipped enough or ready enough for the task set before us. Rather, our call as followers of Jesus is to heed his voice, rely on his strength, and go where he leads.

Read | 2 Corinthians 12:6–10

Reflect

1. Paul was once a Pharisee who persecuted followers of Jesus. Perhaps more than any other apostle, he made the journey to the other side of becoming a believer and then founding many churches. He faced trial after trial, and abuse after abuse, yet he kept spreading the good news. According to this passage, what was sufficient (or enough) for Paul? What was made perfect in Paul's weakness? What do you think this means?

2. Why did Paul say that he could actually boast in his weakness? What effect do you think that attitude had on those to whom he was ministering?

3. Are there any areas in which you feel weak in your faith or not sufficient enough for the task before you? What do you learn from Paul's example in this passage?

4. How could Jesus' words to Paul give you hope in your weakness? How could Jesus' words encourage you each day to have the confidence to go to the other side?

Pray | Ask God to show you how he wants you to go to the other side today. Pray especially that he will give you eyes to see any needs that you might have overlooked. Then ask him to give you the confidence to go to those places, trusting that his strength is all you need for the task.

- Day 5 -

Revelation to Be Had

Have you ever gone on a trip with a group of people you didn't know very well? After spending seven to eight days with them, what changed in your relationship? Most likely, you got to know them more intimately. Traveling with people, eating meals with them, getting lost with them—these are all bonding experiences that reveal people's true colors.

This is what happens when you make the daily decision to go to the other side with Jesus. You begin to see him in a new way. His true self is revealed to you. When you go to the other side with Jesus, there is always revelation to be had. You get to see him work miracles. You get to see him change even the most callous and hardened hearts. You get to see him do what in the natural is impossible! But when you refuse to go to the other side—when you allow fear, doubt, and anxiety to get in the way—you miss this revelation.

There is a fascinating story told in the Old Testament where an army of Arameans had surrounded an Israelite city where the prophet Elisha and his servant were staying. The servant saw all the enemy horses and chariots and cried out in fear, "Oh no, my lord! What shall we do?" (2 Kings 6:15). Elisha calmly replied, "Don't be afraid. . . . Those who are with us are more than those who are with them" (verse 16). The prophet then asked God to open his servant's eyes so that he would receive revelation. When he did this, the servant looked out and saw that the hills were "full of horses and chariots of fire all around Elisha" (verse 17).

It is one thing to read your Bible and attend church and *learn* about who Jesus is. It is something altogether different to *experience* who Jesus is. You can only do this if you venture to the other side where his power, grace, and mercy are on full display. The servant of Elisha was never the same after receiving God's revelation. In the same way, when you go with Jesus to the other side and witness his awe-inspiring power, your life will never be the same.

Read | Matthew 16:13–19

Reflect

1. The disciples had been traveling and ministering with Jesus for some length of time when the events in this passage took place. Yet Jesus must have sensed that at least some of the disciples were unclear as to his true identity. What question did Jesus ask to get them thinking about this? How did the disciples initially respond?

2. Jesus turned the question to his disciples, asking, "But what about you? . . . Who do you say I am?" (verse 15). How did Peter reply to this question? How do you think Peter's personal experiences with Jesus helped him to comprehend Jesus' true identity?

3. What experiences have you had with Jesus that have revealed his identity and character to you? How did this revelation change the way you viewed or understood Jesus?

4. What has Jesus been revealing about himself to you recently? What implications does this revelation have for your faith and how you interact with others?

Pray | Ask Jesus to keep revealing himself to you . . . day by day and every day. Ask him to give you the courage to go to the other side so that you can fully experience who he is and his love for you. Ask him to keep your eyes and heart open to new revelations from him.

For Next Week

Before you meet again with your group next week, read chapter 14 in *The God of the Way*. Also go back and complete any of the study and reflection questions from this personal study that you weren't able to finish.

Schedule

WEEK 2

BEFORE GROUP MEETING	Read chapter 14 in *The God of the Way* Read the Welcome section (page 29)
GROUP MEETING	Discuss the Connect questions Watch the video teaching for session 2 Discuss the questions that follow as a group Do the closing exercise and pray (pages 29–40)
PERSONAL STUDY – DAY 1	Complete the daily study (pages 42–43)
PERSONAL STUDY – DAY 2	Complete the daily study (pages 44–45)
PERSONAL STUDY – DAY 3	Complete the daily study (pages 46–47)
PERSONAL STUDY – DAY 4	Complete the daily study (pages 48–49)
PERSONAL STUDY – DAY 5 (before week 3 group meeting)	Complete the daily study (pages 50–51) Read chapter 15 in *The God of the Way* Complete any unfinished personal studies

The Demoniac

GOD TAKES THE INITIATIVE

When Jesus got out of the boat, a man with an impure spirit came from the tombs to meet him. This man lived in the tombs, and no one could bind him anymore, not even with a chain. For he had often been chained hand and foot, but he tore the chains apart and broke the irons on his feet. No one was strong enough to subdue him. Night and day among the tombs and in the hills he would cry out and cut himself with stones.

MARK 5:2–5

Welcome | Read On Your Own

In the last session, you explored what it meant for Jesus' disciples to go to the other side of the Sea of Galilee. You looked at what the "other side" represents in our day, how God calls us to step out of our comfort zones, and why we need to stay focused on Jesus and rely on his strength. This week, you will continue to travel with the disciples as they land on the eastern shore of the sea and meet a man who had been labeled, defined, and cast aside by society.

This man from the region of the Gerasenes had spent years being defined by his affliction: demon possession. He was so completely consumed by the evil spirits that had come to inhabit his body that he had no idea who he was anymore. But then, he met Jesus. The Savior cut through the labels and revealed the man's true identity: a beloved child of God.

This revelation forever changed the demoniac's life . . . and it will forever change ours as well. After all, we know only too well what it feels like to be consumed by something that has come to define us: fear, power, pride, anxiety, depression, hopelessness, sin, lust. These are attacks from the enemy that we encounter each and every day, and if we are not careful, they can take over and become our identity—an identity we were never meant to have.

As you will see in this week's study, Jesus did not mess around with the demons who had stolen the man's identity. He told them to declare themselves and then cast them out into a herd of pigs. Jesus then restored the man to wholeness and gave him a mission. The man became a new creation . . . no longer a slave to the enemy. He was free to again be part of his family. Free to be loved. Free to be accepted. Free to receive a robe of righteousness.

Connect | 15 minutes

Welcome to session 2 of *The God of the Other Side*. To get things started for this group time, discuss one of the following questions:

- What is a key insight or takeaway from last week's personal study that you would like to share with the group?

— *or* —

- What are some labels that people in our society try to place on others? What are some of the labels that people have tried to place on you?

Watch | 20 minutes

Now watch the video for this session (remember that you can access this video via streaming by following the instructions printed on the inside front cover). As you watch, use the following outline to record any thoughts or concepts that stand out to you.

I. What is the cultural background of the region known as the Decapolis?

A. Jesus, after the feeding of the 5,000, told his disciples to get into a boat and cross to the "other side" of the Sea of Galilee (see Matthew 14:13–22).

1. Meanwhile, Jesus went up on a mountainside to pray. Later that night, a storm arose on the lake that threatened to sink the disciples' small boat (see verses 23–24).

2. Jesus walked on the water to the disciples. Peter got out of the boat when Jesus called out to him but sank when he lost faith. Jesus saved him and hushed the storm (see verses 25–33).

3. The disciples had survived the ordeal of the crossing, but they still had to go to the other side. This was the Decapolis, a place the Jewish people were forbidden to go.

B. The Decapolis was a place where pagan religions were practiced. The history of the region dates back to the time of Joshua and the Israelites conquering the Promised Land.

1. God had instructed the Israelites to completely drive out all the people who inhabited Canaan so they would not be a snare to them (see Deuteronomy 20:16–17).

2. However, there were many people groups who were not conquered. One such group fled to the eastern-northern shore of the Sea of Galilee (modern-day Jordan).

The Roman Legion

The Roman legion was the largest military unit in the Roman army. The size of a typical legion varied throughout the history of ancient Rome, but during the first century, it was typically comprised of 5,600 infantry and 200 *auxilia*. For most of the Roman Imperial period, legions formed the Roman army's elite heavy infantry, with its members drawn from Roman citizens. The *auxilia*, or auxiliary troops, were primarily comprised of non-Roman citizens.[4]

A legion was broken down into *centuries*, which were most often comprised of eighty men. These *centuries* were further divided into ten groups (with eight men in each) who shared a barrack, room, or tent. Six centuries formed a cohort, and ten cohorts made a legion. The first cohort, which was considered the most prestigious, carried the legionary standard and gold eagle (called an *aquila*).[5] The Roman *century* was led by an officer called a *centurion*, who was typically a professional soldier who had worked his way up through the ranks.[6]

Centurions could be identified by a transverse crest (horizontal plume facing the front) and armor and shin guards that were different from the typical soldier. The centurion carried a sword (*gladius*) on his left, a dagger (*pugio*) on his right, and a vine stick (*vitis*) that served as a sort of badge of his rank and with which he disciplined the troops. Some centurions also wore medals of valor (*phalerae*) that they had earned in battles. The provincial governor of the region determined who was worthy to be promoted to the rank of centurion.[7]

When Jesus asked the demon-possessed man for his name, he received the response, "My name is Legion . . . for we are many" (Mark 5:9). Most scholars believe the explanation "for we are many" indicates the reference is meant to be general rather than specific—in other words, that he was not possessed by 5,000 to 6,000 demons, but just that he was possessed by a great host of them. Whatever the number, it was enough to panic 2,000 pigs (see verse 13).[8]

3. The territory had originally been chosen by the tribe of Manasseh during the time of Moses and given to them as their possession (see Joshua 13:29–31).

C. The tribe of Manasseh failed to drive the Canaanites completely out of their land and instead pressed the people that remained into slavery (see Judges 1:27–28).

1. The tribe of Manasseh, in choosing that particular portion of the Promised Land, believed they would always be established in the land and hold it as their possession.

2. However, the very people whom the Israelites failed to conquer—the ones they allowed to stay—fled to that particular region and established themselves there.

3. By the time of Jesus, the region had become an area of pagan worship, which is why the Jews were forbidden to go there. Today, you can visit the location (now called Beit She'an) and see the ruins of all of the pagan temples and related worship sites.

II. What happened after Jesus and the disciples landed in this region?

A. Jesus and the disciples landed in the region of the Gerasenes and were confronted by a demon-possessed man who was naked and covered in blood (see Mark 5:1–5).

1. Jesus is the only one to get out of the boat. The man runs up to him, falls on his knees, and says, "What do you want with me, Jesus, Son of the Most High God?" (verse 7).

2. Jesus asks, "What is your name?" (verse 9). Some believe he was asking the demons to identify themselves, but Jesus already ruled over them and knew who they were.

3. Jesus was asking the *man* to give his name. He wanted the man to get back in touch with his identity and his intrinsic value as a beloved child of God.

B. Jesus received this response: "My name is Legion . . . for we are many" (verse 9).

1. *Legion* means "many." In the Roman army, a legion consisted of 5,000 to 6,000 soldiers. Most commentators say the man was possessed by more than 1,000 demons.

2. Regardless of how many demons inhabited the man, he was completely overrun by them. The demons knew Jesus and begged him to let them remain in the region.

3. The demons begged Jesus to send them into a herd of pigs (see verse 12). Pigs were the most unclean animals in Jewish culture—the most "unkosher" thing they could pick.

C. Jesus allowed the demons to go into the pigs, which were about 2,000 in number. When this happened, the pigs rushed into the lake and were drowned (see verse 13).

1. This is significant because scholars believe that pigs were the primary food source in this region. The death of these 2,000 pigs would have represented a significant loss to the local food supply.

2. Those who were tending the pigs quickly reported what they had seen in the town and the countryside. The people came out to see what had happened (see verse 14).

3. When they arrived, they saw the man delivered from torment—which nobody could make sense of—and the man who had just wrecked their economy. This made Jesus unpopular among the population, and they asked him to leave (see verses 15–17).

III. What is the conclusion to this story of the demon-possessed man?

    A. The people see the man who had formerly been cutting himself with stones "dressed and in his right mind" (verse 15). It was a dramatic before-and-after transformation.

        1. We do not know this man's story or what led him to be possessed by so many demons. But we do know that he became what the God of the Other Side intended him to be.

        2. We can picture Jesus wrapping him in a robe of righteousness. He went from being dressed in filthy rags to wearing clean and pure linens.

        3. The man begs Jesus to allow him to go back with him. But Jesus instructs the man to return to his village and tell everyone what God has done (see verses 18–19).

    B. It would have been incredibly difficult for the man to obey this command from Jesus.

        1. We do not know how long the man had been living in the tombs—but it would have been a long time. He would have endured years of rejection from society.

        2. Jesus was asking the man to do an incredibly difficult task in going back to the people who had scorned him for most of his life. This mission from Jesus represented the man's "other side."

Fishing in the Time of Jesus

Jesus called four of his disciples—Peter, James, John, and Andrew—to leave their fishing trade behind and come follow him. Given this, it is little wonder that the Gospels contain many stories that are connected to the Sea of Galilee and the fishing industry. Fish were abundant in biblical times, and the fishermen of Jesus' day employed special tools to catch them.

Boats. The discovery of a first-century boat (called the "Ancient Galilee Boat" or the "Jesus Boat") indicates that the vessels the fishermen used were around twenty-seven feet long, seven-and-a-half feet wide, and four feet deep. These dimensions imply that the boats of Jesus' day would have held up to fifteen people. The twelve disciples (plus Jesus) would have been cramped and jostled around quite a bit during their encounters with storms.[9]

Nets. When Jesus called Simon and Andrew to be his disciples, he found them "casting a net into the lake" (Mark 1:16). The nets of the time were circular, about fifteen feet in diameter, and comprised of a fine mesh. The fisherman placed lead sinkers around the edges of the net so it would sink to the bottom of the lake. He then held a long line attached to the center of the net with his left hand, gathered the net up in his right hand, and cast it into shallow water.

Hooks. Jesus once instructed Peter to "go to the lake and throw out your line" and "take the first fish you catch" (Matthew 17:27). Such an operation would have required Peter to use some form of metal hook to make the catch. Inscriptions from 700 BC reveal that Assyrian fishermen used hooks and line for fishing. The Romans created networks of small iron pits to sustain the army's demand for swords and spearheads, and hooks were made as a byproduct.

Anchors. Fishermen in biblical times used the anchor in much the same way it is used today. Early anchors were often just large stones or pieces of wood weighed down with stones. Metal anchors were in use by the first century. Anchors could be thrown from either end of the boat (see Acts 27:30). When ships anchored near the shore, they were placed with their stern to the beach and their bow in deeper water, with the anchor being cast down from the bow.[10]

    3. Yet the man obeyed. Later, read in Scripture that when Jesus returned to the region of the Decapolis, so many people believed in him that the crowds were enormous. This was all due to the man's testimony.

  C. Jesus' restoration of this man is a foreshadowing of him restoring our own identity (see Revelation 12:11). Jesus had not yet gone to the cross or ascended to the Father, yet in this story we get a picture of him ruling and reigning over a demonic presence.

    1. This man became one of the first evangelists to the Gentiles. His story gives us hope that we too—as Gentiles—are now included in this great gospel that Jesus brought.

    2. The Jews of Jesus' day had been taught not to leave their homes, synagogues, or culture. They were never to go somewhere where they could be violated by the pagan world. Now, Jesus was making a way for the Gentiles to be grafted into God's family.

    3. No matter where we come from, and regardless of our past, we can all be adopted into God's family. He loves *everyone* and *everything* he ever created.

IV. What does this story of Jesus restoring the demon-possessed man reveal to us today?

  A. One of the key takeaways from this story is that the God of the Other Side reaches out to everyone. There is not one person on the planet whom God does not want to touch.

    1. Everyone has a right—and a choice—to become a part of God's family. We are called to leave the "pew" of our local church and go out and reach the world.

2. This does not necessarily mean that God will call us to some exotic place. However, we are all supposed to be missionaries who spread the message of the gospel.

3. Wherever God calls us to serve, we can be certain that he will equip us for the task.

B. Another important lesson from this story is that God can use *anyone* to fulfill his purposes on earth.

1. Today, we tend to assume the work of spreading the gospel is just for those whom God has "chosen"—for those called to be ministers, evangelists, and missionaries.

2. But the truth is that God uses all kinds of different people to do his work. We need to join together—old and young alike—to work side by side in God's mission to the world.

3. It is only when we move with one purpose that we move ahead. Members of the body of Christ—the church—must "hook arms together" to break through any spiritual opposition in our mission.

4. The demon-possessed man was able to transform a whole culture and unify them around the personhood of Jesus. This is what the church should be doing today.

C. We need to stop leading people off the cliff and instead lead them into the arms of God. We need to stand by one another and help each other fulfill our God-given destinies. We have a message that the world needs to hear . . . and those who encounter Jesus are never the same.

Discuss | 35 minutes

Take some time to discuss what you just watched by answering the following questions. There are some suggested questions below to help you begin your discussion, but feel free to pick any of the additional questions as time allows.

Suggested Questions

1. Ask someone in the group to read aloud Mark 5:1–5. Imagine that you were one of the disciples in the boat that day and you suddenly saw a bleeding man with an "impure spirit" running out of a tomb at you. Do you think you would have gotten out of the boat? Why or why not? How did Jesus respond to the demon-possessed man?

2. Continue reading the story in Mark 5:6–13. Notice that when Jesus asked the man for his name, the demons spoke up instead and identified themselves as "Legion." What does this say about the affliction the man was experiencing and the desperation he was feeling? In what ways can you relate—at least in part—to his circumstances?

3. Now ask someone to read aloud Romans 1:18–20. Paul states that God makes his eternal power and divine nature known in this world. How did Jesus reveal his divine authority over the enemy in the story of the Demoniac? What does this tell you about the authority that Jesus has over any foothold the enemy has established in your life?

4. At the end of the story, we read that the people of the nearby town found the former demon-possessed man "dressed and in his right mind" (Mark 5:15). How did they respond when they witnessed this miracle? Why did they respond in that manner?

Additional Questions

5. Read aloud Mark 5:18–20. What did the restored man beg from Jesus? What did Jesus ask him to do instead? Why do you think Jesus asked him to do this?

6. What was the result of the man's evangelism? Knowing what you do about the region they were in, why is this especially significant for the spreading of the gospel?

7. Jesus told the restored man to go to his "other side" and proclaim the message of the gospel to the community that had cast him out when he was demon-possessed. When have you felt God calling you to return to a community, job, group of friends, or family who once rejected you? What was that experience like? How did Jesus equip you for that particular calling?

8. Read Revelation 12:11. The demoniac was feared and rejected by society. Then he met Jesus and became a living example of God's power through his testimony. How have the testimonies of others impacted you? How could your testimony impact others?

Respond | 10 minutes

Review the outline for the video teaching and any notes you took. In the space below, write down your most significant takeaway from this session.

Pray | 10 minutes

End your time by praying together, asking God to deliver you from any attacks of the enemy in your life. Ask if anyone has any prayer requests to share. Write those requests down in the space below so you and your group members can pray about them in the week ahead.

Name	Request

Personal Study

As you discussed this week, the story of the demon-possessed man living in the Decapolis reveals that Jesus has the power to heal those who find themselves on the "other side." There is no person on this planet whom he is not able, willing, and determined to reach. Regardless of what those in the culture may say, there is also no individual who is "too far gone" for Jesus to heal and restore. As you continue to explore this theme this week, be sure to write down your responses to the questions, as you will be given a few minutes to share your insights at the start of the next session if you are doing this study with others. If you are reading *The God of the Way* alongside this study, first review chapter 14 in the book.

-Day 1-

Get Out of the Boat

The disciples had been through a terrifying ordeal by the time their battered boat reached the eastern shore of the Sea of Galilee. The night before, Jesus had instructed them to get into the boat and "go over to the other side" (Mark 4:35). As they made the crossing, a furious storm arose that nearly swamped the boat. On this occasion, Jesus was with the disciples, sleeping in the stern. He awoke, rebuked the waves, and brought calm to the chaos.

The disciples had witnessed Jesus in his divine glory. Still, when the morning broke, the issue remained of what awaited them when they reached the shore. They had good reason for concern. As you learned in this week's session, the region where they landed (Decapolis) was off-limits for the Jewish people. Had the disciples stepped foot on that soil, they would have been unclean. In addition, when they did land, they were met by a screaming demon-possessed man.

The Gospels make no mention of the disciples getting out of the boat when Jesus approached the man. It is difficult to fault them for this reaction. Most of us would have wanted to row back out into the lake to escape the presence of such a demonic force. When encountered with such a fearful sight, our natural instinct is to just run away. We prefer the safety and security of what the "boat" offers us. So we just stay put.

The Bible reveals that following Jesus always requires us to take bold steps. This means trusting Jesus to lead us instead of putting our trust in the things the world says will give us security—things such as money, relationships, comfort, and success. Whatever we put before our faith in Jesus—whatever we love or worship above him—is what God calls an *idol*.

If we want to go to the other side, we have to release these idols. It is only when we do this that we allow the full power of Christ to work in and through us. It is only when we step out in faith that we experience complete surrender to God and his will for our lives.

Read | Matthew 8:14–22

Reflect

1. Those who witnessed Jesus' miracles were drawn to him, but not all chose to follow him. Consider Jesus' response to the teacher of the law who had evidently witnessed the healing of Peter's mother-in law and said he would follow Jesus "wherever" he went. Why did Jesus respond as he did? What idol was Jesus pointing out in this man?

2. The next man to approach Jesus was a disciple who asked if he could bury his father before following him to the other side of the lake. While it may seem harsh of Jesus to not let this man bury his father, in Jewish tradition, a second burial of the body took place a year after the person's death. This disciple was likely asking Jesus to give him a year before he started following him.[11] Knowing this, why do you think Jesus responded the way he did? What idol was Jesus pointing out in this disciple?

3. What might be some of the idols that are keeping you from getting out of the boat and following Jesus? Why are these people or things so important to you?

4. What would it look like to trust Jesus more than those idols? What would you have to release in order for that to happen?

Pray | Come before God today and ask for his help in surrendering any idols in your life. Ask him to forgive you for holding on to them so tightly and for the courage to let them go.

-Day 2-

Identity Restored

Those who are on the fringes of our modern societies are given many different labels: *homeless, sick, disturbed, mentally ill*. Few people would ever take the time to learn the name of a person living on the streets near their home. It is far easier to simply place a label on them according to their marginalized status rather than get to know them.

The Demoniac in this week's story is known as just that—a demoniac. He was "a man with an impure spirit" (Mark 5:2). In fact, we never learn his name in any of the accounts of his story told in the Gospels. But Jesus did . . . because Jesus asked him.

As noted in this week's teaching, a common misconception is that Jesus was asking the *demons* to give him their names. However, Jesus would have already known the names of the demons because he had all authority over them—and he even gave this authority to his disciples and followers when he sent them out (see Luke 10:19). Rather, Jesus wanted to know the name of the *man*—the one who had been trapped because of his affliction.

When Jesus asked this question, he was revealing that he saw this man as more than one who was possessed or a lost cause. He saw this man as a precious child of God. Simply asking the man's name was a step toward restoring his true identity.

You don't have to be part of a marginalized group to feel labeled. Maybe others have put labels on you that aren't necessarily negative but also don't fully capture who you are: *dependable, hard worker, mom, dad, so-and-so's son or daughter*. It's easy to lose yourself in the labels that others have given you. When you've been known as this one thing for so long, you start to believe that's all you are.

But Jesus doesn't see you this way. He sees the real you. He knows your name (see Isaiah 43:1). He has called you a beloved child of God (see 1 John 3:1). Just like the man in our story, once you've met him, your true identity will be restored.

Read | Luke 8:26–39 and Isaiah 61:10

Reflect

1. Read the descriptions of the demon-possessed man in Luke's Gospel in verses 26–28 and verses 35–36. How do the descriptions of the man differ? Why do you think the people who came were "overcome with fear" (verse 37) when they saw him?

2. Isaiah 61:10 points to God's restoration of Israel and the coming of the Messiah into the world. How does Isaiah describe the clothing the Lord has given him? How could this verse also describe the demoniac and what he was clothed in after meeting Jesus?

3. How have you labeled others in your community? How have others labeled you?

4. If you truly believed that everyone who was in Jesus had received the garment of salvation and a robe of righteousness, how would that change the way you view those you tend to label? How would this change the way you view yourself?

Read | Imagine that you are clothed in righteousness and wearing a garment of salvation. Ask God to help you believe that you have been made new—for you are a new creation! Your true identity is not one someone else gave you. It is the one Jesus gave you: beloved child of God.

— Day 3 —

People Over Projects

As followers of Jesus, we have been called to fulfill God's mission of reaching the lost. But while we strive faithfully to serve in this calling, we often do not always go about it in the right way.

Perhaps you have been on a mission trip where the people you were serving were seen as a project rather than as people. Your goal was to "fix" them or add them to the number of those who became "saved" on your trip. Or maybe you have been a part of a church who had a homeless ministry, but instead of approaching those who were experiencing homelessness in your community with mercy and grace, you approached them as an "issue" that needed to be addressed.

It is also quite likely that at some point in your life you have been on the other side of this equation. Perhaps *you* have been approached as a project by some well-meaning Christians. They wanted to tell you about how to be saved, but they didn't really want to get to know you. They wanted you to get plugged into their church, but they didn't really care about who you were. Their approach lacked what Jesus had in abundance: love for the other person.

When we read Jesus' interactions with individuals in the Gospels, we find that he *always* approached people as people and never as projects. As discussed in yesterday's personal study, he did this in the case of the demon-possessed man by taking the time to ask the man's name. Jesus allowed every interaction he had with others to be led by love rather than an agenda.

When we approach people as projects, we overlook the fact we are interacting with a beloved child of our heavenly Father who has a God-given identity, gifting, and purpose. If we do not have love for the person, we are—as the apostle Paul so eloquently put it—"only a resounding gong or a clanging cymbal" (1 Corinthians 13:1). If we do not take the time to get to know the people we are serving, we are just making discordant noise in this world.

Read | 1 Corinthians 13:1–7

Reflect

1. The spiritual gifts and traits that Paul mentions in this passage—tongues, prophecy, service, sacrifice—are all worthy things for us to pursue and desire to have. But what does Paul say is the secret ingredient for them all? Why do you think this is the case?

2. Consider the ways in which Paul defines *love* in verses 4–7. How should this description inform how you approach ministry and how you use your spiritual gifts?

3. When has someone treated you like a project rather than a person? How did this make you feel—and how did you respond to the person who treated you this way?

4. Think about someone who truly loves you as a person and does not have a predetermined agenda in their interactions with you. How has that person's example impacted you? Who do you sense that Jesus is calling you to love like that today?

Pray | Thank Jesus for his love and that he does not see you as a project or something to be fixed. He simply loves you, just as you are. Allow yourself to sit in this love. Let it wash over you.

-Day 4-

Dealing with the "Unclean"

I t wasn't just the disciples who worried about being unclean if they set foot on the other side. We too are worried about people and places that could defile us. While what we consider unclean differs and varies among people groups and cultures, the intense desire to avoid what is "unclean" is in us all. In fact, it is an ancient instinct we inherited from our ancestors.

Psychologist Dr. Richard Beck explains this ancient instinct as *disgust*—the feeling we get when we don't like a certain food or find ourselves in an unsanitary bathroom.[12] This same feeling comes up when we encounter someone whom we consider to be unclean— someone who is sick, sinful, mentally ill, sexually promiscuous, and the like. We form tight circles in our communities that seek to keep the unclean out and the clean in. We scapegoat those who might defile us. We do the opposite of what Jesus did during his time on earth.

Jesus had no such reservations in approaching the unclean. He touched those afflicted with diseases such as leprosy and restored them (see Mark 1:40–42). He healed not only the demon-possessed man in the Gerasenes but also a demon-possessed boy (see 9:25–27). He accepted invitations from sinners and tax collectors and shared meals with them in their homes (see 2:13–16). He was not concerned that the place or the person would defile him.

The disciples undoubtedly watched these events in complete shock. After all, they were Jews and had followed the Levitical cleanliness laws for their entire lives. But Jesus was making a statement with his actions. He was establishing a new law: him and him alone. Gone were the old codes and standards of purity. What made someone clean was *Jesus*.

Sadly, we often operate under the old code. We hold people at arm's length and judge whether they are worthy to be included in our circle, community, and church. The ancient instinct of disgust is still in us. But when it arises, we must remember how Jesus treated those who were marginalized and unclean—and ask for the compassion to do the same.

Read | Luke 19:1–10

Reflect

1. The Jewish people in Jesus' day had no love for tax collectors and regarded them as "sinners." These were fellow Jews who worked for the Romans who had occupied their land, and so they were generally seen as traitors. Furthermore, tax collectors received no wages from the Romans, so their earnings came from keeping a portion of the revenues they collected. Many tax collectors, like Zacchaeus in this story, were dishonest in this practice and took far too much for themselves. How did Jesus encounter Zacchaeus? What did Jesus say when he saw him?

2. How did Jesus demonstrate his willingness to go to the "other side" where his fellow Jews were not willing to go? How did the people respond to him?

3. Who is considered unclean in your community—the people who are typically shunned or avoided—and why? How have you ever been treated as unclean?

4. Who is someone you typically avoid who is in need of God's love? What are some practical ways that you could show that person (or group of people) mercy?

Pray | End your time in prayer. Ask God to forgive you for ever considering others unclean. Thank Jesus for making you clean. Ask him to give you his heart of mercy and compassion.

-Day 5-

The Power of a Testimony

We all know the power of a good story. You probably remember the first time you read *that* book or saw *that* movie—the one with a storyline so powerful that it changed you and has stuck with you all these years. This is true of our testimonies as well. In fact, maybe it was somebody's testimony that led you to Jesus. The person's story was so compelling that you wanted to experience what they had experienced for yourself.

Testimonies have the power to change societies. In 1904, a young investigative writer named Upton Sinclair spent seven weeks undercover working as a meatpacker in Chicago. At the time, there was no legislation controlling either the quality of the meat being packed or the conditions of the workers—both of which were appalling. Two years later, when Sinclair published his book on his research called *The Jungle*, it created such an outcry among the public that the government enacted the first of a series of Pure Food and Drug laws.[13]

The Demoniac certainly had a story to tell after he encountered Jesus. Right after he was healed, he begged to go with Jesus in the boat to follow and minister with him. But instead, Jesus said to him, "Go home to your own people and tell them how much the Lord has done for you, and how he has had mercy on you" (Mark 5:19). So the man did as Jesus had instructed and shared his story in the Decapolis. As a result, "All the people were amazed" (verse 20).

That is the power of your testimony. You might think that you do not have anything to offer by way of evangelism. You're not a biblical scholar or an impressive orator. You don't have one of those dramatic before-and-after salvation stories that you've heard so many others share. Know that none of this is required to be a spreader of the good news! If you have a story—and who doesn't?—you have something to offer. You can be an evangelist simply by telling a friend what Jesus has done in your life. The word of your testimony has more power than you know.

Read | 1 John 1:1–4 and Revelation 12:10–12

Reflect

1. Scholars believe that the letter of 1 John was written toward the end of the disciple John's life. What does John state in the opening of his letter about his testimony and personal experiences of being with Jesus? Why do you think he makes it such a point to begin with this statement before he tells his readers anything else?

2. The book of Revelation is John's account of a prophetic vision he received about the end times, when Satan would finally be defeated and Jesus would reign. In this passage, the "accuser" is Satan. What does John say that our testimony has the power to do?

3. Who in your life has shared a personal testimony that changed your view on something? What did that person say that was so powerful?

4. Spend some time writing down your testimony if you've never done it. How has Jesus changed your life? How have you seen God recently working in your life?

Pray | Ask God who you could share your testimony with this week. Ask him to place that person in front of you. Then pray for him to give you the courage to share!

For Next Week

Before you meet again with your group next week, read chapter 15 in *The God of the Way*. Also go back and complete any of the study and reflection questions from this personal study that you weren't able to finish.

WEEK 3

BEFORE GROUP MEETING	Read chapter 15 in *The God of the Way* Read the Welcome section (page 55)
GROUP MEETING	Discuss the Connect questions Watch the video teaching for session 3 Discuss the questions that follow as a group Do the closing exercise and pray (pages 55–66)
PERSONAL STUDY – DAY 1	Complete the daily study (pages 68–69)
PERSONAL STUDY – DAY 2	Complete the daily study (pages 70–71)
PERSONAL STUDY – DAY 3	Complete the daily study (pages 72–73)
PERSONAL STUDY – DAY 4	Complete the daily study (pages 74–75)
PERSONAL STUDY – DAY 5 (before week 4 group meeting)	Complete the daily study (pages 76–77) Read chapter 16 in *The God of the Way* Complete any unfinished personal studies

The Samaritan Woman

GOD OFFERS NEW LIFE

The Samaritan woman said to him, "You are a Jew and I am a Samaritan woman. How can you ask me for a drink?" (For Jews do not associate with Samaritans.) Jesus answered her, "If you knew the gift of God and who it is that asks you for a drink, you would have asked him and he would have given you living water."

JOHN 4:9–10

Welcome | Read On Your Own

In the last session, you saw how Jesus healed the demon-possessed man who was living among the tombs on the other side of the Sea of Galilee. You looked at how Jesus allowed the legion of demons in the man to go into a herd of pigs. You also explored how Jesus restored the man's identity and the impact that the man's testimony had on the people in the area.

This week, you will travel with the Messiah as he goes to the "other side" to reach another person in need of God's grace. In the Gospel of John, we read that Jesus traveled to the town of Sychar in Samaria. It was around noon when he arrived, the day was hot, and he was thirsty. So he sat down beside a well and, because he had no way to draw the water, waited for the visitor he was expecting to arrive. In a short while, a woman appeared and came to the well.

Jesus would use his physical thirst and the life-giving water in the well to describe his mission on earth of bringing living water to those who are spiritually thirsty for God. Just as water is essential to our physical health and well-being, so the living water that Jesus offers is essential for our spiritual health and well-being. The offer of Jesus is to give us "rivers of living water" (John 7:38) through the indwelling power of the Holy Spirit.

In this session, you will take a closer look at the conversation that Jesus had with the Samaritan Woman. You will see how he broke cultural barriers just to meet with her and told her so many things about her life that she declared him to be a prophet. You will also explore how her interaction with the Messiah forever changed her life and compelled her to become one of the first missionaries of the gospel to the people of the "other side."

Connect | 15 minutes

Welcome to session 3 of *The God of the Other Side*. To get things started for this week's group time, discuss one of the following questions:

- What is a key insight or takeaway from last week's personal study that you would like to share with the group?

— or —

- When was a time you felt intense thirst? How did it feel when you finally got a drink of water?

Watch | 20 minutes

Now watch the video for this session. As you watch, use the following outline to record any thoughts or concepts that stand out to you.

I. Who were the Samaritans—and why did the Jewish people try to avoid them?

    A. The Bible relates a story in which one day Jesus decided to take a journey from Judea to Galilee. We read that in making the trip, "he had to go through Samaria" (John 4:4).

        1. What is interesting about this statement is that Jesus should *not* have gone through this region. It represented the "other side" for most Jewish people—and they avoided it.

        2. Of course, Jesus is the Son of God and can go anywhere he wants. But in this case, he "had" to go through Samaria because he wanted to meet a specific person.

        3. Most Jews in Jesus' day did not travel through Samaria when traveling from Judea to Galilee, even though it was a shortcut. They avoided it because of the Samaritans.

    B. The conflict between the Jews and the Samaritans went way back in their shared history.

        1. The nation of Israel was comprised of twelve tribes. Ten tribes inhabited the land to the north, while two tribes (Judah and Benjamin) were in land to the south.

        2. God had instructed his people to not allow the Canaanites to remain in the land. But they only partially obeyed this command, and so remnants of these people groups remained. The Israelites often fell under their influence and worshiped their gods.

        3. The nation of Israel divided into two kingdoms, consisting of the ten tribes in the north (called Israel) and the two tribes in the south (called Judah). When Israel fell to the Assyrians, the people began to intermarry with the Assyrians.

The History of Samaria

"But a Samaritan, as he traveled, came where the man was; and when he saw him, he took pity on him" (Luke 10:33). Samaria was located in the central region of Palestine in Jesus' day. It was bordered on the north by Galilee, by Judea on the south, by the Mediterranean Sea on the west, and by the Jordan River on the east. It extended about forty miles from north to south and about thirty-five miles from east to west. The ancient city of Shechem (near modern-day Nāblus), located in the middle of Samaria, served as the crossroads and political center of the region.

The history of Samaria begins with the Israelite conquest of the Promised Land under Joshua. The region was given to the tribes of Ephraim and Manasseh, but they were not able to completely possess the land, and pockets of Canaanite resistance persisted until the time of King David, when the entire region was brought together into the United Kingdom. Following the death of King Solomon, the ten northern tribes (including those of Samaria) separated from the two southern tribes and formed the separate kingdom of Israel.[14]

Omri, the sixth king of Israel, bought a hill in the Valley of Shechem and erected the city of Samaria, which because its capital (see 1 Kings 16:23–24). Eventually, this name was applied to the entire region. Ahab, the son of Omri, built a temple to Baal there.[15] The northern kingdom was often politically stronger than the southern kingdom of Judah, and witnessed greater economic development, which made it a target of the Assyrians. In 722 BC, the Assyrian king Shalmaneser V conquered the nation and subjugated its people. The Assyrians imported other conquered people groups into the region, "diluting" the Jewish population.[16]

Over time, this led to the development of a unique religious belief system called "Samaritanism." The Samaritans built their own temple on Mount Gerizim, where they believed Moses instructed the Israelites to build an altar to the Lord. They also held that only the Torah was the authoritative law of God and rejected the rest of the Hebrew Bible. This led to tensions between the Jews and the Samaritans that persisted into Jesus' day, as evidenced by a story in the Gospel of John. When some of the Jews in Jerusalem wanted to criticize Jesus, they called him "a Samaritan and demon-possessed," all in the same breath (see 8:48).[17]

4. This was forbidden according to God's law (see Deuteronomy 7:3–4). So we see a continuing evolution of where there is trouble in the land because the Israelites didn't obey God.

C. There was also a long history of division between the Jews and the Samaritans over the issue of worship.

1. The Jewish people worshiped God in the temple in Jerusalem. The Samaritans worshiped where their forefathers had worshiped (see 1 Kings 12:25–33).

2. The Samaritans also narrowed down what they considered to be the law of God. They held that only the Pentateuch (Genesis–Deuteronomy) had any authority. Furthermore, they claimed that only their copy of the Pentateuch was the original version.

3. Yet Jesus, in spite of this conflict and hostility, determined to enter into "enemy territory" because there was one specific woman at a well whom he needed to meet.

II. What did Jesus say to the Samaritan woman at the well that forever changed her life?

A. Jesus arrived in Sychar in Samaria around noontime. It was the hottest time of the day and Jesus was tired. So he sat down at a place called Jacob's Well (see John 4:5–6).

1. Jesus then waited in expectancy. He had what we call today a "word of knowledge." He knew a woman was about to arrive who was about to have the encounter of her life.

2. It would have been uncommon for women in that time to draw water at noon. The typical time for this task was early morning or later afternoon, when it was cooler.

3. The Samaritan Woman picked this time because she wanted to avoid the other women. She had a past and was filled with shame. But Jesus knew her secrets!

B. The woman was surprised when she saw Jesus sitting at Jacob's Well. But Jesus was not in the least bit surprised. He asked the woman for a drink of water (see verse 7).

    1. The woman said, "You are a Jew and I am a Samaritan woman. How can you ask me for a drink?" (verse 9). This tells us about her personality . . . she was a fighter.

    2. It is most likely that she had to be a fighter just to survive in society. Women during this time—in the patriarchal culture of the day—had absolutely no rights.

    3. A woman at this time was not considered to have the same value as a man. So the Samaritan Woman would have been dependent on a man just to survive.

C. Jesus reveals to the Samaritan Woman that he knows she has been married five times and that the man she is currently living with is not her husband (see verses 17–18).

    1. When we read this statement from Jesus, we tend to assume that it means she made her living as a prostitute. But this is not necessarily the case.

    2. We have to remember that women during this time did not have the right to divorce. So the five husbands in this woman's history had either divorced her or died.

    3. In many ways, her situation was like that of Naomi and Ruth, after their husbands died in Moab. The Samaritan Woman had to live with a man just to survive.

III. What impact did the Samaritan woman's testimony make on the world?

    A. The woman returned to her village after the encounter with Jesus and said, "Come, see a man who told me everything I ever did. Could this be the Messiah?" (verse 29).

        1. The Samaritan Woman is listed in the historical record of the Greek Orthodox Catholic Church, where her name is given as Photini.

        2. It is said she had five children, and all of these children came to accept Jesus as the Messiah. There is a record that her daughter led Nero's daughter to salvation.

        3. It is also written that Photini was the greatest evangelist in that region. She brought the gospel, through her five children, to everybody.

    B. Jesus delivered this woman from shame and from labels that others had placed on her. He did not allow their differences to get in the way of his restoring her identity.

        1. In the dialogue between the Samaritan Woman and Jesus, she often pointed out their differences. She first pointed out that Jesus should not be speaking with her because she was a woman and a Samaritan and he was a man and a Jew (see verse 9).

        2. Later, she points out the differences between Jews and Samaritans in regard to the proper place to worship (see verse 20). Jesus says that soon she will not care about this, because a time is coming when people will "worship the Father in the Spirit and in truth" (verse 23).

        3. Jesus is giving her the message of salvation. Everything changes for her when she realizes that she has encountered God. She can't help but share what Jesus has done.

Symbolism of Water in Scripture

When Jesus met the woman at the well, she said to him, "You are a Jew and I am a Samaritan woman. How can you ask me for a drink?" (John 4:9). Jesus did not answer this particular question but instead used her reference to water to reveal a spiritual truth: "If you knew the gift of God and who it is that asks you for a drink, you would have asked him and he would have given you living water" (John 4:10). Water actually symbolizes many different things in Scripture.

Water = Troublesome Times. Water can symbolize the trials in life that come to all human beings. King David wrote, "Let all the faithful pray to you while you may be found; surely the rising of the mighty waters will not reach them" (Psalm 32:6). In some instances, water also represents enemies who attack and need to be overcome: "He drew me out of deep waters. He rescued me from my powerful enemy, from my foes" (2 Samuel 22:17–18).[18]

Water = the Spirit of God. In the Gospel of John, we read that Jesus stood in the temple and said, "Let anyone who is thirsty come to me and drink. Whoever believes in me, as Scripture has said, rivers of living water will flow from within them." John adds, "By this he meant the Spirit, whom those who believed in him were later to receive" (7:37–39).

Water = Eternal Life. In both the Old and New Testaments, water is used to represent salvation and eternal life, which God offers to humankind through faith in his Son. Isaiah writes, "With joy you will draw water from the wells of salvation" (12:3). In Jesus' encounter with the Samaritan Woman, he said, "Whoever drinks the water I give them will never thirst. Indeed, the water I give them will become in them a spring of water welling up to eternal life" (John 4:14).

Water = God's Word. Water sometimes also symbolizes the spiritual cleansing that comes with the acceptance of God's offer of salvation. Paul writes, "Christ loved the church and gave himself up for her to make her holy, cleansing her by the washing with water through the word" (Ephesians 5:25–26). The water that does the cleansing of the bride, the church, is directly tied to God's Word. Ezekiel also writes, "I [God] will sprinkle clean water on you, and you will be clean; I will cleanse you from all your impurities and from all your idols" (36:25).[19]

C. Suddenly, this woman who went to the well at noontime to avoid the scorn of others is now sharing the message of Jesus with everyone she meets (see verses 28–30).

    1. The people of her village—the ones who wanted nothing to do with her—hear the message of salvation from her and come to believe in Jesus (see verse 39).

    2. This is the Holy Spirit at work. When even a person rejected by society declares the truth of Jesus, the Holy Spirit is catalytic in moving people's hearts to believe.

    3. The Holy Spirit uses even those with horrible backgrounds for God's glory. People see how their lives have been magnificently transformed and say, "God is real."

IV. What does the "living water" that Jesus offers to the Samaritan Woman symbolize?

A. Jesus said to the woman, "If you knew the gift of God and who it is that asks you for a drink, you would have asked him and he would have given you living water" (verse 10).

    1. Water was of incredible importance in Israel. The land is basically a desert. But God had promised to bring springs of water to the desolation (see Isaiah 43:20).

    2. The heat at places like the Dead Sea—the lowest place on the planet—is especially oppressive. So the people in Jesus' day knew the importance of having water.

    3. Water was not only necessarily for people's survival but also for the survival of crops and animals. Water was the most precious commodity in Israel.

B. Jesus tells the woman that those who are spiritually thirsty will find life in him and will never thirst again (see John 4:13–14). They will discover their identity in Jesus. They will discover the purpose of their lives for which God put them on this planet.

    1. The apostle Paul talks about the cleansing of the church and ties it directly to God's Word (see Ephesians 5:25–26). Jesus is the "Word" who was with God (see John 1:1). So everything in our Bibles is "living water"—the living Word of God.

2. Living water is also found in encounters with the Spirit of the living God. We have the Bible as our source of living water, but we have also been given the Holy Spirit (see Acts 1:4–5). The Holy Spirit indwells us and gives us the wisdom and counsel of God.

3. Jesus said, "Whoever believes in me, as Scripture has said, rivers of living water will flow from within them" (John 7:38). This is an indication of the power of the Holy Spirit.

C. When we are moving in tandem with the Holy Spirit—in partnership because of Jesus— we will lead a life in which miracles flow out of it.

1. We should expect miracles to happen every day! We can expect the Holy Spirit to move when we pray. The important part for us is just to be willing to take the risk.

2. We need to adopt the posture of Jesus and pray, "Father . . . not my will, but yours be done" (Luke 22:42). If we really believed that, we would step out in faith and pray, "Lord, if you want to touch someone's life through me today, just lead me in that way."

3. The Samaritan Woman drank of the living water the Savior gave and, in turn, became living water for others. Her testimony about Jesus changed an entire region.

4. Some years ago, springs of fresh water were discovered bubbling up from the base of the Dead Sea. You may feel like the Dead Sea today—lifeless and desolate—but God has not abandoned you. He knows your story and has a purpose for you.

Discuss | 35 minutes

Take some time to discuss what you just watched by answering the following questions. There are some suggested questions below to help you begin your discussion, but feel free to pick any of the additional questions as time allows.

Suggested Questions

1. The nation of Israel divided into two kingdoms—north and south—after the death of Solomon. The northern kingdom, known as Israel, was invaded and captured by the Assyrians. After this happened, the people began to intermarry with the Assyrians, leading to the formation of two distinct people groups: Jews and Samaritans. (You can read the full story in 2 Kings 17:24–41.) Despite this history with the Samaritans, Jesus walked through Samaritan territory, even though most Jews avoided it at all costs. Why did he do this? What does this tell you about Jesus' character?

2. Ask someone in the group to read aloud John 4:1–10. What are your first impressions of the Samaritan Woman based on this part of the story? How would you describe her personality based on her interactions with Jesus when he asked for some water?

3. Now read aloud John 4:11–26. When Jesus said that he could provide living water, it understandably confused the woman at the well. She pointed out that Jesus had no way to draw water even from the well in front of him—so how could he provide living water? How did Jesus respond? What does "living water" represent for us?

4. John relates another situation in which Jesus told the people, "I am the bread of life. Whoever comes to me will never go hungry, and whoever believes in me will never be thirsty" (John 6:35). How is this similar to what he said to the Samaritan Woman? What is Jesus saying about himself by stating he is the "water" and "bread" of life?

Additional Questions

5. Ask someone to read the conclusion of the Samaritan Woman's story in John 4:27–42. What effect did the living water have on the Samaritan Woman's testimony? What does this tell you about the power of your testimony when you have the Holy Spirit?

6. God said to his people, "I will make rivers flow on barren heights, and springs within the valleys. I will turn the desert into pools of water, and the parched ground into springs" (Isaiah 41:18). When has God brought water to a dry and parched area of your life—whether you felt dry spiritually, emotionally, relationally, or otherwise?

7. The apostle Paul wrote, "Christ loved the church and gave himself up for her to make her holy, cleansing her by the washing with water through the word, and to present her to himself as a radiant church, without stain or wrinkle or any other blemish, but holy and blameless" (Ephesians 5:25–27). What connection does Paul make between *water* and the *word* in this passage? How is the *word*—the Word as scripture and the Word as Jesus—like water in our lives? How have you personally experienced this?

8. When the Samaritan Woman experienced the living water of Jesus, she could not help but share how it had changed her life—even with those in her town who had likely scorned her. What impact did the woman's testimony have on the people in that region? What does this say about the importance of following Jesus to the "other side"?

Respond | 10 minutes

Review the outline for the video teaching and any notes you took. In the space below, write down your most significant takeaway from this session.

Pray | 10 minutes

End your time by praying together, thanking God for giving you the living water found in Jesus. Ask if anyone has any prayer requests to share. Write those requests down in the space below so you and your group members can pray about them in the week ahead.

Name	Request

Personal Study

As you discussed this week, Jesus offers his life-giving water to all who are thirsty—Jews and Gentiles alike—and restores their God-given identities. The Samaritan Woman had certainly been labeled by her culture as an outsider. The Jewish culture from which Jesus came said that he should consider her an outsider as well. Instead, Jesus went out of his way to reach her and include her in God's family. As you explore these themes this week during your personal study time, write down your responses to the questions, as you will be given a few minutes to share your insights at the start of the next session if you are doing this study with others. If you are reading *The God of the Way* alongside this study, first review chapter 15 in the book.

-Day 1-

A Long-Running Feud

Perhaps the most infamous feud in the history of the United States was the one that broke out between two families in 1863. While the true origins of the feud are obscure, some believe it started when Rand'l McCoy of Kentucky suspected that the family of "Devil Anse" Hatfield of West Virginia had stolen one of his hogs. Whatever the reason, the Hatfield-McCoy feud would last for nearly thirty years and claim more than a dozen lives from both sides.[20]

Yet the feud between these two families is no match for the one that took place during the time of Jesus—a conflict that had gone back hundreds of years. It all started when the united kingdom of Israel split into two separate kingdoms. Each nation went their own way and were conquered by different enemies, leading to two people groups (the Jews and the Samaritans) who shared certain customs and beliefs but otherwise were very different.

For instance, the Samaritans believed the true place of worship was not the temple in Jerusalem but a temple on Mount Gerizim. They had a different version of the Pentateuch (the first five books of the Hebrew Bible) than the Jews and rejected the writings of the major and minor prophets. To the Jewish people, Samaritans were worse than the Gentiles.[21]

Most Jews would not be caught in Samaritan territory. Although walking around it increased the duration of their journey from Judea in the south to Galilee in the north, they preferred that to taking a shortcut through "enemy" territory. Most Jews . . . but not Jesus.

In the story of the Samaritan Woman, Jesus did not simply stop at a well and ask for a drink of water. He stopped at a well in a *Samaritan* village and asked a *Samaritan woman* to get him a drink. In doing so, Jesus was making a statement. He was willing to go to a hated people group of the Jews, converse with them, and tell them they were loved by God. What hundreds of years of animosity had built, Jesus tore down with a single conversation.

Read | John 4:39–41, Acts 1:4–8, and Acts 8:4–8

Reflect

1. According to John 4:39–41, how did the Samaritans who responded to the woman's testimony feel about Jesus? How do you think Jesus felt about the Samaritans?

2. Luke records some of the last instructions that Jesus gave to his followers in Acts 1:4–8. They were to wait in Jerusalem until they were baptized with the Holy Spirit. Why do you think Jesus then specifically told them to be his witnesses in Samaria?

3. One disciple who took Jesus at his word was Philip. According to Acts 8:4–8, what happened when he went to Samaria? How did the people respond to the gospel?

4. Who is a "Samaritan" in your life—a person or people group you are at odds with, whether that's religiously, politically, or relationally? How would Jesus treat your Samaritan? How might he be calling you to do the same?

Pray | Thank God for the Samaritans in your life. They are a reminder that no one is beyond Jesus' love or forgiveness. Ask God to help you have mercy and compassion on those in your life you don't understand or simply don't like. Ask him to help you see them in a new way.

Day 2

Fully Known

The ancient Greek playright Aeschylus wrote that "rumors have wings." When rumors go unchecked, they can quickly "fly" through the air and land on the ears of eager listeners who assume them to be truth. Perhaps you have been the victim of a rumor. Lies and half-truths were spread about you that affected how people saw you and who they thought you were. Or perhaps you have helped spread a rumor, whether you knew it was truth or not.

It is evident when you read the story of the Samaritan Woman that many rumors had been spread (and believed) about her. The women of that time did not go for water at noon—in the heat of the day—but went in the early morning or late afternoon when it was cooler. The only reason the Samaritan Woman went to the well at noon is because she knew she would be alone . . . away from the stares and hushed gossip of her community.

It soon becomes clear why she is avoiding them. Jesus reveals that she had been married five times and was currently living with a man who was not her husband. Modern-day readers often take this to mean that she was a prostitute. However, as noted in this week's teaching, women in the New Testament did not have the right to divorce. So she was likely either abandoned by her five husbands or they had died. As a woman, she did not have rights and needed the provision of a man. While we don't know the details of her living arrangement with the man not her husband, we know that without him, she would have been destitute.

Jesus knew all about her past, but this didn't compel him to judge or scorn her. Instead, he offered a view of how God saw her—as his own child. The Samaritan woman went from being misunderstood and gossiped about to being fully known. This is how Jesus sees you as well. He knows your story—your *full* story—and he accepts you as you are. He offers you the same gift that he offered the Samaritan woman on that day: living water.

Read | John 4:27–30, Jeremiah 23:23–24, and Colossians 3:1–4

Reflect

1. A tremendous change occurs in the Samaritan Woman after her encounter with Jesus. Whereas before she wanted to hide from people, she now sought them out to share her good news. While the Samaritans and the Jews had many differences, they were both waiting for a promised Messiah. So how did the community respond to her news?

2. The Samaritan Woman was astounded when Jesus revealed parts of her past that she wanted to hide. What does the Lord say in Jeremiah 23:23–24 about what we can "hide" from him? Why do you think we still try to hide parts of our past from him?

3. Paul reveals what our identity should now be in Colossians 3:1–4. What does it mean that we have "died" and our lives are now "hidden with Christ in God"?

4. How has Christ made you feel known or understood in a way that your family, friends, or community did not understand? What is an area of your life where you still feel misunderstood—and how could you invite Jesus into that place?

Pray | In your prayer time today, meditate on the words of Psalm 139:1–18, which serves as a beautiful reminder of how intimately God knows each and every one of us. Read it aloud or to yourself. Pause on the verses that stick out to you. Let them sink in as truth.

— Day 3 —

A New Covenant

Jesus didn't meet with the Samaritan woman at any old well. He met her at Jacob's Well (see John 4:6). This location is historically significant for God's people. Traditionally, they believed it to be the place where Jacob first inhabited the Promised Land (see Genesis 33:18-19). He later gave this land to his son Joseph (see 48:21–22), whose sons were the founding tribes in the southern region of Israel (Ephraim and Manasseh), which would later become Samaria.[22]

In other words, Jacob's Well was a big deal to the Samaritans. It was holy ground that represented tradition and the law. The law, to Jews and Samaritans alike, was paramount.

This context sheds some light on an otherwise peculiar part of Jesus' conversation with the Samaritan Woman. When Jesus said to her, "If you knew the gift of God and who it is that asks you for a drink, you would have asked him and he would have given you living water," the woman responded, "Sir . . . you have nothing to draw with and the well is deep. Where can you get this living water? Are you greater than our father Jacob, who gave us the well and drank from it himself, as did also his sons and his livestock?" (John 4:10–12).

Notice that the Samaritan Woman was asking Jesus if he was greater than their father Jacob. In other words, "Are you saying that you are greater than our tradition and the law?" Jesus answered, "Everyone who drinks this water will be thirsty again, but whoever drinks the water I give them will never thirst. Indeed, the water I give them will become in them a spring of water welling up to eternal life" (verses 13–14).

Jesus was offering a new covenant. The old covenant gave the Israelites the law. The new covenant gave them Jesus: the embodiment of grace and mercy. What the Samaritan Woman likely only partly understood then, we understand in full today. Jesus brought a new way, a living water that we only have to drink once, and we will never thirst again.

Read | Hebrews 9:11–15 and Romans 10:1–4

Reflect

1. The high priests of Israel in Old Testament times offered the blood of animals as a sacrifice to God. According to Hebrews 9:11–15, how did Jesus replace that sacrifice? What was he able to obtain for us by offering his own life as a sacrifice?

2. Paul writes that "Christ is the culmination of the law so that there may be righteousness for everyone who believes" (Romans 10:4). The old covenant gave the Israelites the law. But what was Jesus offering them through the new covenant?

3. Jesus offered the Samaritan Woman grace at Jacob's Well—a place that symbolized the law. When have you experienced the grace of Jesus in an area of your life that was once ruled by the law—by rigid rules or expectations?

4. Where do you need grace today—an area where you are still operating under the law?

Pray | End your time in prayer. Thank Jesus that you are no longer a slave to sin or to the law. There is a new and better way, one only made possible through his sacrifice. Ask him to help you experience grace where you need it most today.

-Day 4-

Living Water

It is not an understatement to say that water represents life. Approximately fifty-five to sixty percent of the human body is actually made up of water. It carries nutrients and oxygen to the cells. It carries wastes out of the body. It helps convert food into energy and protects and cushions vital organs. It regulates body temperature, lubricates joints, and moistens oxygen for breathing. Humans can last up to six weeks without food—but only one week without water.[23]

Given the importance of water to the human body, it is little wonder that it is used so frequently throughout Scripture. In fact, the word *water* is used 722 times in the Bible, more than *faith* or *hope*.[24] It symbolizes difficulties (see Isaiah 43:2), salvation (see Isaiah 12:3), purity (see Ephesians 5:26), and—as you learned this week—eternal life and the Holy Spirit. As Jesus said, "Whoever drinks the water I give them will never thirst. Indeed, the water I give them will become in them a spring of water welling up to eternal life" (John 4:14).

We understand the power of water in our physical lives. But do we accurately equate this to the power that Jesus and the Holy Spirit have in our spiritual lives? Do we see Jesus as powerful, living, active, and vital to our being? Or has Jesus become a subject to study, a person to whom we occasionally pray, or someone we hear about from the pulpit on Sundays? Is Jesus alive to us like a mighty ocean or dead to us like a barren wasteland?

So often we settle for a ho-hum faith. A dry version of the life-giving one that God has intended for us. We forget the living water inside us is the power of the Holy Spirit. This isn't to say that every moment of our journey has to be fun and exciting. There are plenty of dreary days and dry moments. But even in those seasons, the offer by the well still stands. No matter how dry or dreary life has become, Jesus is still there, offering us his living water.

Read | Revelation 21:5–6 and Revelation 22:1–5

Reflect

1. The vision John relates in these passages from the book of Revelation provide a picture of what life will be like when Jesus returns and we are reunited with God in a new heaven and a new earth. What is water used as a symbol for in these passages?

2. Revelation 22 is titled "Eden Restored" in some translations of the Bible. It describes how God will restore the earth to its original form—just as it was originally in the garden of Eden before the fall. What role does John say that water plays in the restored Eden? What does this tell you about the power of water and the Spirit?

3. Paul writes, "We were all baptized by one Spirit so as to form one body—whether Jews or Gentiles, slave or free—and we were all given the one Spirit to drink" (1 Corinthians 12:13). What does it mean to "drink" from the Spirit? How does the power of the Holy Spirit flow through followers of Jesus and give them life?

4. What areas of your spiritual life feel dry today? How could the "water" of the Holy Spirit bring abundant life and growth to those particular areas?

Pray | Thank Jesus for his gift of living water. Ask him for help in any area of life that feels dry. Ask him to reveal his power to you so you feel his living water flowing through your spiritual life.

– Day 5 –

Let the River Flow

Sometimes, we can feel that our impact on the world for Jesus is like the impact that a drop of rain has on the earth. Sure, we know that God has given each of us a story—a testimony—of what he has done for us that he wants us to share. But with so much skepticism, doubt, and disbelief in the world, we wonder what impact our little "drop" of water can actually make.

What we don't tend to realize is how God can use even the seemingly insignificant things in this world for greatness in his kingdom. Just consider that drop of water that falls from the sky. It sinks into the earth, where it joins with other drops of rain to nourish crops in a field. It collects into larger pools of water that ultimately form into rushing rivers. It even fills vast oceans and seas that have mighty waves. Our God can use our stories—and the stories of others—in powerful ways that we could never imagine.

Our part is simply to *say* what Jesus has done for us—to allow the living water within us to flow out and give life to others. This is what the Samaritan Woman did. As soon as she experienced Jesus for who he was—the Messiah—she left her water jar at the well, went back to her town, and told them what she had seen and heard (see John 4:28–29). She shared the living water with others and, as a result, many of them became believers.

Our faith should never stop with us. Still, we can be reluctant to share our testimony and our gifts. Perhaps, as we've discussed in previous sessions, we don't think our story is powerful enough. Or maybe we don't think our gifts are interesting enough. But we have to remember that Jesus said, "If you have faith as small as a mustard seed, you can say to this mountain, 'Move from here to there,' and it will move" (Matthew 17:20).

There is nothing too small or too insignificant that God can't use for greatness when it is surrendered to him. So share your story with others—and let the living water flow!

Read | 1 Corinthians 12:1–31

Reflect

1. In this passage, Paul discusses the spiritual gifts that are given to followers of Jesus through the indwelling of the Holy Spirit. He tells his readers that he is providing this explanation of the gifts so that they will not "be uninformed" (verse 1). According to verses 4–6 and verse 11, what is similar about the gifts of the Spirit?

2. Paul lists several of the gifts of the Spirit in verses 8–10. Why do you think God provides so many different types of gifts in his church?

3. Notice the analogy of the human body that Paul uses in verses 12–19. He states that every part of the body, no matter how small or insignificant it may seem, serves a vital function and a purpose to the whole. How is this similar to the spiritual gifts?

4. What gifts do you believe God has given you to serve your fellow brothers and sisters in Jesus? How are you using those gifts to share the living water with others?

Pray | Thank God for instilling the power of his Spirit within you. Thank him for making you unique with unique gifts to share with others. Ask him to give you the courage to use your gifts to spread his message. Ask him specifically how and where you could do that this week.

For Next Week

Before you meet again with your group next week, read chapter 16 in *The God of the Way*. Also go back and complete any of the study and reflection questions from this personal study that you weren't able to finish.

WEEK 4

BEFORE GROUP MEETING	Read chapter 16 in *The God of the Way* Read the Welcome section (page 81)
GROUP MEETING	Discuss the Connect questions Watch the video teaching for session 4 Discuss the questions that follow as a group Do the closing exercise and pray (pages 81–92)
PERSONAL STUDY – DAY 1	Complete the daily study (pages 94–95)
PERSONAL STUDY – DAY 2	Complete the daily study (pages 96–97)
PERSONAL STUDY – DAY 3	Complete the daily study (pages 98–99)
PERSONAL STUDY – DAY 4	Complete the daily study (pages 100–101)
PERSONAL STUDY – DAY 5 (before week 5 group meeting)	Complete the daily study (pages 102–103) Read chapter 17 in *The God of the Way* Complete any unfinished personal studies

The Prodigal Son

GOD WELCOMES US HOME

"The son said to him, 'Father, I have sinned against heaven and against you. I am no longer worthy to be called your son.' But the father said to his servants, 'Quick! Bring the best robe and put it on him. Put a ring on his finger and sandals on his feet. Bring the fattened calf and kill it. Let's have a feast and celebrate. For this son of mine was dead and is alive again; he was lost and is found.' So they began to celebrate."

LUKE 15:21–24

Welcome | Read On Your Own

In the last session, you looked at the story of the Samaritan Woman. You saw how Jesus went to the "other side" of what was considered culturally acceptable for Jewish people by traveling to Samaria. You explored how Jesus revealed his identity as the Messiah to this woman and offered her living water. In the process, he restored her identity as a child of God.

In this session, you will learn about two brothers who also struggled with their identities. These men were not actually real people but characters in one of Jesus' best-known parables. The first son was a wayward or "prodigal" young man who one day went to his father, asked for his inheritance, and then proceeded to squander it all on wild living. The second son, who was the oldest, was a dutiful young man who stayed by his father's side and worked alongside the servants out in the fields in the hopes of earning his father's favor.

The younger son sought his identity in experience. The older son sought his identity in performance. All the while, they were missing out on a relationship with their loving father.

Each of us can relate in some way to one of these brothers. Some of us are like the younger son. We value experience, adventure, and everything that this life has to offer. Others among us can relate to the older son. We value performance, achievement, and the satisfaction that we believe hard work promises to us. But as the story of the Prodigal Son reveals, at the end of the day, each of these avenues will only leave us feeling empty inside.

All the father wanted from his sons—and all that God wants from us—is a *relationship*. It is only through relationship with him that we can find our purpose and meaning in life. When we rest in that, we can stop striving—or partying—and find out who we really are in him.

Connect | 15 minutes

Welcome to session 4 of *The God of the Other Side*. To get things started for this week's group time, discuss one of the following questions:

- What is a key insight or takeaway from last week's personal study that you would like to share with the group?

— *or* —

- Think about the first time you heard the story of the Prodigal Son. How was the story taught to you? Which character was the focus?

Watch | 20 minutes

Now watch the video for this session. As you watch, use the following outline to record any thoughts or concepts that stand out to you.

I. What do we know about the setting for the parable of the Prodigal Son?

    A. The parable of the Prodigal Son is a famous story that we all think we know well.

        1. However, there are many details in the story that would have been evident to Jesus' listeners that are more hidden to us. As the rabbis would say, "There's more!"

        2. There is such wealth to be gained in studying the actions of the father and both sons . . . though traditionally the focus has been on the younger son (the prodigal).

        3. Yet there is also a lot that we can learn from the older brother. It all depends on how we were raised and where we find our significance.

    B. The parable of the Prodigal Son appears only in Luke's Gospel and was told when Jesus was in Capernaum.

        1. Capernaum is on the northwestern shore of the Sea of Galilee. Jesus was teaching there—perhaps in one of the synagogues that archaeologists have discovered.

        2. Rabbis used imagery in their stories that people could touch, see, hear, smell, and feel—that was common and relatable to them. Jesus did the same in his stories.

        3. It was the spirit of storytelling that made everything come to life for the people. The power of a good story can change the culture—and Jesus was a master storyteller.

Families in Biblical Times

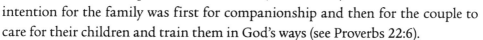

In ancient Israel, the family was the basis of society and the cornerstone on which it was built. The Bible reveals that God formed the first human family by joining Adam and Eve together as husband and wife. The Lord said, "It is not good for the man to be alone. I will make a helper suitable for him" (Genesis 2:18). God's intention for the family was first for companionship and then for the couple to care for their children and train them in God's ways (see Proverbs 22:6).

The twelve tribes of Israel, established during the days of Moses, originated from a family unit—the sons of Jacob and Joseph. By the time of Jesus, families were not as autonomous or even as strong as they had been during the era of the patriarchs, but they nevertheless remained an important foundation of Jewish society. Certain religious ceremonies, such as the Passover, had to be performed in a family. The link between religion and families was so strong that in the Gospels and Acts, we find that fathers who turned to Jesus for salvation brought with them their entire households (see John 4:53; Acts 16:34; 18:8).[25]

The father was the head of the family. In ancient times, his sons and daughters were considered his property, and he had the absolute right to sell them as slaves or even condemn them to death (see Genesis 22:1-19; Exodus 21:1-11; Judges 11:29-39). This was no longer the case in Jesus' day, yet the father was still regarded as the ruler of the house. Everything the family possessed fell under the command of the father to do with as he saw fit. This means that in the story of the Prodigal Son, the father had every right to sell off his assets and give the proceeds to his sons. Neither of the two boys really had any say in the matter.

Sons were expected to support their parents when they grew old and then give them a proper burial. For this reason, a couple typically hoped to have many sons (see Psalm 127:4-5). The firstborn son always held the greatest place of honor within the familes. He was expected to assume control of the household from his father, so it was typical for him to receive a double portion of the inheritance (see Deuteronomy 21:17). Sons were commanded under God's law to honor their father and mother (see Exodus 20:12), which is why the disrespect the Prodigal Son showed to his father would have been considered so scandalous.[26]

C. One point that will be important to remember in the story is that Capernaum (where the father lived) is close to the Decapolis (where the Prodigal Son would travel).

    1. The road that runs from Capernaum around the northern tip of the Sea of Galilee is five miles. So what was called the "faraway place" in the story was just five miles away.

    2. It is possible to even see the Decapolis from Capernaum on a clear day. So the father, from his home, would have been able to look out at the place where his son had gone.

    3. A modern equivalent in our day would be if a child ran away from home and went to Las Vegas—a place where a person could easily go and lose his or her soul.

II. What did the Prodigal Son request of his father—and why was it so scandalous in that time?

A. Jesus begins by introducing the characters: a man and his two sons (see Luke 15:11).

    1. This was an agricultural culture, so they had animals, vineyards, and fields. They were "working the farm" when the younger son approached his father with a request.

    2. The younger son asks his father to give him his inheritance (see verse 12). This would have been a shock to Jesus' Jewish listeners in this culture, because the younger son, in essence, was making this declaration to his father: "I wish you were dead."

    3. Sons never received an inheritance until after their father had died. So the son was saying that he would rather have his father's money instead of his presence in his life.

B. In that culture, the oldest male received a double portion of the inheritance.

1. The oldest son, when the father died, became patriarch of the family. So it made sense for him to receive more of the inheritance because he was the new family provider.

2. So, in this story, this means that the younger son would receive one-third of his father's estate and the older brother would receive two-thirds of everything.

3. Jesus states that the father "divided his property between them" (verse 12). Scholars who study this story believe this means that the father granted the younger son's request.

C. The story of the Prodigal Son was written for us. The way we find our value is found in the actions of the two sons. The way we find God is found in the nature of the father.

1. Scholars believe that the father not only granted the younger son's request (one-third of the estate) but also gave the older son his inheritance (two-thirds) at the same time.

2. This is speculation, but it makes sense that the older son would not have been left out of the equation. The older son was living with the father anyway, so it would not mean that the family would cast the father out if he gave his sons the inheritance.

3. If the older son was included in the division of the estate, it magnifies the things we see in the story. The older son received his inheritance but was still working the land.

III. What do we learn from the Prodigal Son's actions in leaving and then returning home?

A. The younger son receives his money and sets off "for a distant country" (verse 13).

1. Once there, he squanders his money on high-rolling living, prostitutes, and everything else. But he soon finds himself destitute (see verses 13–14).

2. The younger son finds himself working in the Decapolis (see verse 15). This region was blasphemous in nature to the Jews due to all the pagan worship practices.

3. Even worse, he has to take a job tending pigs—an animal that was unclean under Jewish law. He is so hungry that he desires to eat the pods (see verse 16).

B. The Prodigal Son soon comes to his senses and realizes that even his father's workers are treated better than he is currently being treated (see verse 17).

1. The son knows the nature of his father as well, so he knows that he can return back home. The father in this story is the symbol of our loving heavenly Father (see John 3:16).

2. The younger son, due to his shame, expects to be rejected by his father. He comes up with a plan for his father to take him back as a servant (see Luke 15:18–19).

3. However, the father is watching for his younger son, and when he sees him approaching from a long way off, he runs to him (see verse 20). No man of modesty would have done this in that day—it was considered vulgar in the culture—but the father did not care.

C. The Prodigal Son, just as he had planned, confesses to his father that he has sinned greatly against him and is unworthy to be called his son (see verse 21).

1. The father is so filled with joy that he doesn't respond. Instead, he instructs his servants to bring him a robe, a ring (probably from his own hand), and sandals (see verse 22).

The Problem with Pigs

Unclean animals, like pigs, play a role in three of the stories covered in this study. In the account of the Demoniac, pigs were the unfortunate hosts of the legion of demons that Jesus sent out of the man. In the tale of the Prodigal Son, pig-feeding was the only occupation the young man could find after running away from home and spending all his father's money. Later, in the narrative of Peter and Cornelius, we will see that unclean animals are featured prominently in a vision that Peter is given—and how that vision changed the history of the church.

The laws that God established for his people concerning which animals were to be considered clean or unclean are found in Leviticus 11. At the beginning of that passage, the Lord said to Moses, "You may eat any animal that has a divided hoof and that chews the cud" (verse 3). He went on to say, "The pig, though it has a divided hoof, does not chew the cud; it is unclean for you" (verse 7). The split hooves symbolized outer purity, while an animal that chewed its cud symbolized inner purity. While pigs might look clean on the outside, the Jewish people knew they were unclean because of what was happening on the inside.

Over time, the pig—from a traditional Jewish mindset—became the ultimate unkosher animal. The Jewish readers of Matthew's Gospel would have seen the irony of the demons going into the pigs in the story of the Demoniac. They would have understood that the Prodigal Son's decision to feed pigs was indicative of just how desperate he had become and to what degree he had compromised his traditional Jewish values. This would have been further emphasized by the young man's desire to fill his stomach with the pods that the pigs were eating. These would have been the seeds of the carob tree that were used for this purpose.[27]

As Rabbi Jason Sobel notes, "The Hebrew word for *pig* is *hazir*, which has the Hebrew root word spelled *chet-zayin-resh*. The Hebrew verb meaning *return* uses the same consonants. This suggests that someday the pig will return and become kosher. The pig will become on the inside what it appears to be on the outside. This doesn't mean that the Torah is incorrect. It means that the pig will be transformed. It will chew its cud and become a new creation (see 2 Corinthians 5:17). Breakthrough begins with repentance and return. To fully experience a transformation, the younger son had to go through barrenness to obtain a breakthrough."[28]

2. The robe was a symbol the father still considered him as his son. The ring was a sign of royalty and kinship. He called for a fatted calf to be killed (see verses 23–24).

3. When the father had sandals put on the younger son's feet, it was an indication that his identity had been restored. Only the slaves did not wear shoes.

IV. What do we learn from the older son's reaction to his brother's homecoming celebration?

A. All this time, the older brother has been toiling in the fields and resenting his younger brother. He is not pleased when he hears sounds of celebration (see verses 25–28).

1. The telltale sign of how the older son viewed his father is revealed in his statement, "All these years I've been slaving for you and never disobeyed your orders. Yet you never gave me even a young goat so I could celebrate with my friends" (verse 29).

2. The father responded that he had always been with his older son and he could have asked for anything and received it (see verse 31). This is an indication that they had no relationship. The other brother found his value working with the slaves in the field.

3. The older brother was working for his father but did not have a relationship with him. We often do the same with God. We do things *for* him but don't really *know* him.

B. The older son was resentful and compared his situation to that of his brother. The person who finds significance in performance often judges, is critical, and compares.

    1. The younger son found his value in experience. He could not find any identity in himself until he went out and experienced everything that life had to offer.

    2. These are two indicators of personality types in our culture today. Both of the sons were off base in their thinking, but both also had an orphan heart. They did not find their value in their father or in their father's love. They found their value in their circumstances and in their performance.

    3. Regardless of our upbringing, we can all relate in some way to the younger son (who valued experience) and the older son (who valued performance).

C. We can be high performers in nature but still have an intimate relationship with God.

    1. If we by nature value performance, we can know that we will not become couch potatoes just because we fall in love with God. We will actually become the best version of ourselves.

    2. The Bible says that God views us as a "special possession" (1 Peter 2:9) just as we are—outside of our performance. We are the most valuable thing in his creation.

    3. God valued us so much that he sent his only Son to die for our sins—not because of all the things we can do for him, but simply because of his incredible love for us.

Discuss | 35 minutes

Take some time to discuss what you just watched by answering the following questions. There are some suggested questions below to help you begin your discussion, but feel free to pick any of the additional questions as time allows.

Suggested Questions

1. Ask someone to read aloud Luke 15:11–16. When the younger son asked his father for his share of the inheritance, he was basically saying, "I wish you were dead." In spite of this affront, the father honored his request. What does this tell you about the younger brother's character? What does this say about the father's character?

2. It didn't take long for the younger son to go out and squander all the money he had received. He soon found himself destitute when a famine hit the land and had to hire himself out to feed pigs—an animal that was considered unclean to the Jewish people. When have you seen a situation like this happen in your life or in the life of a loved one?

3. Ask someone to read Luke 15:17–24. The younger son eventually came to the place where he recognized that even his father's servants had a better life than the one he was currently living. What plan did he concoct in his mind to get his father to agree to take him back? What does this imply that he knew about his father's nature?

4. Ask someone to read the conclusion to the story in Luke 15:25–32. While the younger brother was away from home, the older son was out working in the fields. In what was he finding his identity? What did the father say to him when he complained that he had never received even a young goat so that he could celebrate with his friends?

Additional Questions

5. The father responded to the Prodigal Son's return by instructing his servants to put a robe around him, place a ring on his finger, and give him sandals to wear on his feet. What do each of these items symbolize? When have you experienced acceptance from God or someone in your life the way the father accepted back his younger son?

6. The apostle Paul wrote, "A man reaps what he sows" (Galatians 6:7). How was this truth manifested in the lives of the older and younger brother in this story?

7. John wrote, "If we confess our sins, he is faithful and just and will forgive us our sins and purify us from all unrighteousness" (1 John 1:9). How do you see the truth of this verse play out in the story of the younger son? What does that say about how God forgives and restores us when we confess our transgressions?

8. Jesus said, "Take my yoke upon you and learn from me, for I am gentle and humble in heart, and you will find rest for your souls. For my yoke is easy and my burden is light" (Matthew 11:29–30). How does this passage speak to those who struggle with finding their identity in works and performance? What is Jesus offering you today?

Respond | 10 minutes

Review the outline for the video teaching and any notes you took. In the space below, write down your most significant takeaway from this session.

Pray | 10 minutes

End your time by praying together as a group, thanking God for being your perfect (and patient) heavenly father. Ask if anyone has any prayer requests to share. Write those requests down in the space below so you and your group members can pray about them in the week ahead.

Name   Request

Personal Study

In the group time this session, you explored how the story of the Prodigal Son is a story about what we value and where we try to find our identities. The younger son found his value in experiences. The older son found his value in performance. Neither son found his value in the relationship with his loving father—and as a result, each son had an "orphan heart." As you continue to explore these themes in this week's personal study, be sure to write down your responses to the questions, as you will be given a few minutes to share your insights at the start of the next session if you are doing this study with others. If you are reading *The God of the Way* alongside this study, first review chapter 16 in the book.

Day 1

The Prodigal

The *rebel*, the *wayward one*, the *black sheep*—we have a lot of nicknames for the archetype of the Prodigal Son in the parable Jesus told. We often equate him to a person who has walked away from the faith, or rebelled against a parent, or engaged in some kind of reckless living. But the actual definition of the word *prodigal* is a bit more specific than this broader definition: "characterized by profuse or wasteful expenditure: lavish."[29]

This understanding of the word *prodigal* makes complete sense when we consider what the younger son in the story did with the inheritance that his father graciously provided to him. As we read, "The younger one said to his father, 'Father, give me my share of the estate.' . . . Not long after that, the younger son got together all he had, set off for a distant country and there squandered his wealth in wild living. After he had spent everything, there was a severe famine in that whole country, and he began to be in need" (Luke 15:12–14).

The younger son wanted to experience everything the world had to offer. But he found out that everything the world had to offer was expensive! When a famine then hit the region, making food scarce and even more expensive, the younger son found that he had no recourse but to work as a hired hand feeding pigs. He was so hungry that he wished he could fill his stomach with the disgusting pods that the swine were eating.

It is a familiar tale: a person pursues worldly possessions and passions only to be left feeling empty as a result. Money does not buy happiness, nor does it buy a sense of worth or value. Although the Prodigal Son had a loving father, he had an orphan heart. He took his father's love and acceptance for granted and looked for it elsewhere. We often do the same. We know that we have a loving heavenly Father who wants to have a relationship with us. But we choose to look to other places for fulfillment . . . and end up feeling empty as a result.

Read | Matthew 6:19–21 and Romans 6:19–23

Reflect

1. In Matthew 6:19–21, Jesus tells a parable about the types of "treasures" that we should be storing up for ourselves. What does Jesus say happens to the treasures that we store up in heaven? What are some examples of heavenly treasures?

2. According to Romans 6:19–23, what were we "slaves" to before we knew Jesus? What are we slaves to now? What free gift do we receive as a result?

3. When have you put your identity in money or worldly possessions? Why are—or were—these things so important to you?

4. Considering the passages you have just read, how does God feel about your money or your possessions? What *really* makes you valuable to him?

Pray | End your time in prayer. Be honest with God about the places you put your worth and your identity. Ask him to restore a truer sense of who you are in him. Offer gratitude for his Word, which is richer than honey and better than gold.

–Day 2–

The Older Brother

While many of us might have a hard time relating to the actions and attitude of the younger son, we can all relate in some way to the older brother. In our Western culture, we value success, performance, and hard work. There is even a prevailing belief that the harder you work, the more value you have as a person. The more successful you are, the more revered you are as an individual. The better you perform, the greater the applause from others.

These values are perfectly embodied in the character of the older brother. Unlike the younger son who ran off to have fun, the older brother stayed behind at the homestead and toiled in the field. He remained in close proximity to his father, but as the events unfold, it is clear the two are miles apart in terms of relationship. So it is that when the younger brother returns home and the father decides to throw him a party, the older son is resentful, bitter, and upset. "All these years I've been slaving for you and never disobeyed your orders," he says. "Yet you never gave me even a young goat so I could celebrate with my friends" (Luke 15:29).

The older brother represents the perfectionist and performer within each of us. The one who earns his place in the world by doing more and doing it better. The one who finds value in slaving away in the hopes that all his hard work will somehow please the father. The one who thinks that if he does more, works harder, and performs more perfectly, he will be loved.

This is *not* how the love of God works. We already have God's love. We don't have to earn it. We can rest in that truth. As the father told the older brother, "My son . . . you are always with me, and everything I have is yours" (verse 31). God's love is *already ours*. Any earning or striving we are doing for him is in vain, rooted in our cultural beliefs of what makes us worthy and valuable. Jesus came to offer something so much better to us.

Read | Titus 3:3–8 and Ephesians 2:4–9

Reflect

1. Paul states in Titus 3:3–8 that we once lived in rebellion to God but now, because of Jesus, have been reconciled with him. However, this is not because of any works that we have done. How does Paul say that we became a part of God's family?

2. Paul writes in Ephesians 2:4–9 that it is the love and mercy of God that saved us from sin and rescued us from spiritual death. Why is it important for us to recognize that it is through God's grace we are saved and not through any works we have done?

3. What are some ways in the past that you have tried to earn God's love or acceptance? Why do you think you do these things rather than resting in the promise of grace?

4. What would it look like for you to come to Jesus and find your rest in him?

Pray | Today, simply rest in God's love. Envision coming before Jesus and accepting the gift of grace and rest that he offers. Let yourself feel loved and accepted by him just as you are.

— Day 3 —

The Father

There is one more character in the parable of the Prodigal Son that we need to consider: the *father*. When you think about your own earthly father, different thoughts, feelings, and reactions may rise up within you. Perhaps your father was kind, loving, and forgiving, just like the one in Jesus' parable. But maybe your dad was stern and angry or cold and distant. Or perhaps he was not present at all. When you try to imagine him, nothing comes to mind.

Whatever type of father (or lack thereof) you grew up with, you likely see God in a similar light. If your father was stern and angry, you likely picture God as a judgmental taskmaster. If your father was cold and distant, you likely see God as indifferent toward you. Even if your father by nature was kind and loving, he was still human, which means that at some point in life he did something to disappoint you. No earthly father is a perfect father.

However, this is not the case with God. He is a *perfect* heavenly Father. In the same way the younger and older brothers accurately represent us (and our values), the father in this story accurately represents our Father in heaven. So if you are wondering what God is like and what it means that he is perfect, this is a great parable to consider. The father exhibited compassion, love, and acceptance even when his sons were completely undeserving of it.

This is how your heavenly Father feels about you. He shows compassion to you, rather than anger. He accepts you, rather than asking you to live up to a certain standard. He loves you just as you are and guides you with discipline when you need it. You don't have to earn his love. Your Father is a safe place where you can come as you are, rather than cleaning up beforehand.

God proved this to you by sending his Son to pay the price of your sin so you could forever be with him. So regardless of how you view your earthly father, let this story restore your faith in your heavenly Father. For you have a good Father.

Read | Matthew 5:43–48 and 1 John 4:15–21

Reflect

1. Jesus told his followers, "Love your enemies and pray for those who persecute you, that you may be children of your Father in heaven" (Matthew 5:44–45). What was Jesus saying about the nature of God the Father in giving his followers this instruction?

2. Notice that Jesus also instructs his followers to "be perfect . . . as your heavenly Father is perfect" (verse 48). Jesus is clearly stating here that unlike our earthly fathers, our heavenly Father is always kind, always good, always loving. What do you think Jesus was saying when he instructed his disciples to try and be "perfect" like this?

3. God is not only perfect but he is also love. Love is at the core of his being—it is integral to his very nature—and he wants his followers to model that same kind of love. What does John say in 1 John 4:15–17 happens to those who acknowledge Jesus is the Son of God? How is God's love made complete within us?

4. Considering how the father treated his sons in the parable, how do you think God feels about you? Is this easy or difficult for you to believe about him? Why?

Pray | Spend some time today with your good Father. Thank him for having compassion on you and loving and accepting you just as you are. Ask him to convict you regarding any inaccurate pictures of him that you have in your mind. Ask him to help you understand who he really is.

− Day 4 −

The Robe, Sandals, and Ring

When the father saw his youngest son walking down the road on his way back home, he was not upset or disappointed. He did not chastise his son for not returning sooner, for essentially wasting his inheritance, or wish any type of ill will on him. Instead, he had the exact opposite reaction! He ran out to meet his youngest son, threw his arms around him, and kissed him. He then gave his wayward son who had returned home three items: a robe, a ring, and sandals.

This suggests the younger brother was destitute—that he had neither his own robe nor sandals. Yet these items also hold historical and biblical significance. As mentioned during this week's teaching, the robe was a sign of righteousness, the ring a sign of kinship and royalty, and the sandals a sign the son was no longer a slave (as only slaves did not wear sandals).

The father wasn't simply clothing his youngest son . . . he was restoring the young man's true identity. The son was no longer a slave on someone else's pig farm, and he would not be a slave at his father's house. Instead, he would be restored to his place in the family. After all that he had done, he would be considered righteous and worthy of his father's love.

The prodigal son had gone off searching for himself. He thought he would find his identity out in the world, doing what he pleased. But it wasn't until he returned to his father's home that he found out who he really was: a beloved child and member of his father's household. The items that his father so generously bestowed on him were a physical representation of this love—symbols that left no doubt in the son's mind who he was.

God does not want us to doubt our identity. Through Jesus, we are members of his family. He has restored our identity to us. We can walk confident in the knowledge that we too wear the robe of righteousness, the ring of kinship, and the sandals that signify our freedom.

Read | Isaiah 61:10, Haggai 2:20–23, and Galatians 4:6–7

Reflect

1. What does Isaiah's new robe represent in Isaiah 61:10? How did this robe cause Isaiah to react? According to Haggai 2:20–23, what is the significance of a signet ring?

2. According to Galatians 4:6–7, how has Jesus changed our identity? How do these verses help you understand the significance of the robe, ring, and sandals?

3. When have you received one of these gifts from God: a robe that restored your righteousness, a ring that declared you were his, or sandals that signified you were no longer a slave but free in Jesus? How did this gift change you?

4. What promise do you need most from God today—the robe, the ring, or the sandals? Why that particular promise?

Pray | Thank God for his gifts. Even when you have run away from him, as soon as you return he is ready and waiting with the robe of righteousness, the ring of belonging, and the sandals of freedom. Each of these gifts is yours today and every day. Thank him for making this possible.

-Day 5-

Our Restless Hearts

Jesus gave this invitation to his followers: "Come to me, all you who are weary and burdened, and I will give you rest" (Matthew 11:28). The instruction sounds simple enough for us to follow. We simply go to Jesus when we feel weary and burdened, and he promises to give us his rest. But in reality, letting go and resting in our relationship with God is a difficult part of the Christian life.

The reason for this is because we are so accustomed to working for what we want, earning others' affection and praise, and feeling the pressure to pull ourselves up by our bootstraps when things get tough, that simply allowing ourselves to be children of God can feel impossible. It requires surrender. It requires humility. It requires us to confess that all our good deeds and all our personal accolades are not who we are at our core—and these can be hard to release.

We may wonder who we are if we let go of these things. But as stated in this week's session, "You will not become a couch potato just because you fall in love with God. You will actually become the best version of yourself . . . the person you were created to be."

The younger and older brother wanted to know who they were, but they failed to see that they didn't need to go anywhere or do anything to find this out for their lives. Their identity was right where they were—at home with their father. However, instead of resting in this truth, they were restless, one in his work and the other in his debauchery. They both lacked a relationship with their father and, therefore, didn't know who they were.

We find our true selves when we get to know God and allow him to get to know us. As the church father Augustine once wrote, "You have made us for yourself, O Lord, and our hearts are restless until they rest in You."[30] Our hearts will not find rest until we find our peace in the Father.

Read | Psalm 23:1–6

Reflect

1. This psalm was written by David, who was a shepherd before he was a king. What restful images and descriptions are depicted? What does this tell you about God?

2. David understood that the Lord was his shepherd who guided every step of his life. What are some of the ways that David saw God leading him?

3. What does this psalm suggest about David's relationship with God? What was it like?

4. Think about the accolades or accomplishments that most define you. How would it feel to let go of those things and find your rest in God? Why would it feel that way?

Pray | Meditate on Psalm 23 during your prayer time. Underline any images or descriptions that stick out to you. Then simply talk to your Good Shepherd and listen for his voice.

For Next Week

Before you meet again with your group next week, read chapter 17 in *The God of the Way*. Also go back and complete any of the study and reflection questions from this personal study that you weren't able to finish.

WEEK 5

BEFORE GROUP MEETING	Read chapter 17 in *The God of the Way* Read the Welcome section (page 107)
GROUP MEETING	Discuss the Connect questions Watch the video teaching for session 5 Discuss the questions that follow as a group Do the closing exercise and pray (pages 107–118)
PERSONAL STUDY – DAY 1	Complete the daily study (pages 120–121)
PERSONAL STUDY – DAY 2	Complete the daily study (pages 122–123)
PERSONAL STUDY – DAY 3	Complete the daily study (pages 124–125)
PERSONAL STUDY – DAY 4	Complete the daily study (pages 126–127)
PERSONAL STUDY – DAY 5 (before week 6 group meeting)	Complete the daily study (pages 128–129) Read chapter 18 in *The God of the Way* Complete any unfinished personal studies

Cornelius and Peter

GOD BREAKS DOWN BARRIERS

Peter went up on the roof to pray. He became hungry and wanted something to eat, and while the meal was being prepared, he fell into a trance. He saw heaven opened and something like a large sheet being let down to earth by its four corners. It contained all kinds of four-footed animals, as well as reptiles and birds. Then a voice told him, "Get up, Peter. Kill and eat." "Surely not, Lord!" Peter replied. "I have never eaten anything impure or unclean." The voice spoke to him a second time, "Do not call anything impure that God has made clean."

ACTS 10:9–15

Welcome | Read On Your Own

In the last session, you explored the parable of the Prodigal Son and looked at the different ways in which we try to find our identity. Some of us, like the younger son, seek to find our purpose through experience. Others among us, like the older son, try to find our value through performance. All the while, our heavenly Father is seeking to enter into a relationship with us so that he can give us the identity we crave—as his beloved sons and daughters.

This week, you will learn how God gave this identity to a group of people the Jewish believers were not expecting: the *Gentiles*. Today, we recognize that the gospel is available to all who put their faith in Jesus. However, back in the days of the early church, this idea was nothing short of radical. This is because the Jewish believers—like all the other Jews of their day—considered the Gentiles to be unclean.

The Jews who put their faith in Jesus continued to engage in many of the religious rituals that they had learned over the course of their lives. So, in their minds, if a Gentile wanted to join the church, that person had to basically become "Jewish" by engaging in those same practices. Even the disciples, like Peter, held onto this view after Jesus ascended into heaven.

So you can imagine Peter's surprise one day when God turned this understanding completely upside down. He did this by sending a vision to Peter that altered his concept of what the Lord considered "clean" and by sending messengers to his home from a Gentile named Cornelius. As the story unfolds, it becomes clear that God had a plan for both men that would change the trajectory of the church, making it possible for Gentiles to not only be followers of "the Way" but to also be considered equal to the Jews in God's eyes.

Connect | 15 minutes

Welcome to session 5 of *The God of the Other Side*. To get things started for this week's group time, discuss one of the following questions:

- What is a key insight or takeaway from last week's personal study that you would like to share with the group?

— or —

- What are some rules or rituals you practice that you feel are important in your faith? Why those particular rules and rituals?

Watch | 20 minutes

Now watch the video for this session. As you watch, use the following outline to record any thoughts or concepts that stand out to you.

I. How are we introduced to the story of Cornelius in the book of Acts?

   A. The story of Cornelius, the first known Gentile convert, is pivotal in church history.

     1. Cornelius' story is unique because it reveals how God breaks down all social barriers and all the categories in which we tend to place people today.

     2. Cornelius was a Roman centurion stationed in Caesarea (see Acts 10:1–2). King Herod, a genius architect, had a harbor built there that was a wonder of the ancient world.

     3. The harbor allowed Caesar's ships to arrive from Rome and bring soldiers. Herod also had a palace there where Paul would later be taken as a prisoner (see 23:23)

   B. One day at around 3:00 in the afternoon, an angel of the Lord visits Cornelius (see 10:3).

     1. God sends his angels concerning us (see Psalm 91:11–12). We have angels assigned to our destiny . . . though some of us are not anywhere near our destiny.

     2. Cornelius asks the Lord what he wants from him, and the angel says God is aware of his prayers and gifts to the poor (see Acts 10:4). Cornelius is seen as a righteous man.

     3. Cornelius is not yet a follower of Jesus, though he lives like one. The angel states that God is aware of how he leads his life and remembers him.

History of
Caesarea Maritima

It is believed that the city which would become Caesarea Maritima was first established by Straton I of Sidon (c. 365–352 BC) as a Phoenician colony and trading village. At the time, the settlement was named "Straton's Tower," which was possibly a variation of the name for the Phoenician god Astarte. In 90 BC, the Jewish ruler Alexander Jannaeus conquered the settlement and absorbed it into the Hasmonean Kingdom (a short period of Jewish independent rule). In 63 BC, the Romans came into power and laid hold of the territory. Roman Emperor Augustus Caesar then gave the settlement, and its neighboring coastland, to King Herod.

The city would undergo vast renovations under Herod's rule. He built a palace, aqueducts (to bring water from springs in the northeast), an arena, a marketplace, bathhouses, a temple dedicated to Caesar and Rome, and other prominent buildings. Yet the main focus of his construction efforts was a deep-sea harbor, called the Sabastos (*Augustus* in Greek), that was begun in 22 BC and not completed until 10 BC. The builders of the port used an ingenious method of mixing volcanic ash, salt, and water to form concrete that was then poured into wooden molds. These were sunk to the sea floor to provide supports for the harbor.

When the harbor was finished, Herod dedicated it and the city to Emperor Augustus. He renamed the settlement Caesarea Maritima, or "Caesarea by the Sea," to honor his patron and to distinguish it from other similarly named cities (such as Caesarea Philippi located at the base of Mount Hermon in northern Israel). After Herod's death, the city became the residence of Judea's Roman commissioners and the provincial capital of Judea. Ultimately, the city grew to a size of more than 125,000 people and became the largest city in the province of Judea.[31]

Caesarea Maritima appears several times in the book of Acts. As noted in this session, it was the home of Cornelius (see 10:1). Paul landed in the city after his second missionary journey (see 18:22) and visited Philip the Evangelist there after his third missionary journey (see 21:8–9). The prophet Agabus met Paul there (see 21:10–11). After Paul's arrest, he spent many years in Caesarea Maritima (see Acts 23–26) before finally leaving for Rome (see 27:1–2).

C. The angel instructs Cornelius to send messengers to Simon Peter (see verse 5).

   1. The angel gives Cornelius instructions as to where Peter can be found in the city of Joppa: "He is staying with Simon the tanner, whose house is by the sea" (verse 6).

   2. Cornelius does not hesitate. He calls two of his servants and a soldier, tells them everything that happened, and sends them to Joppa (see verses 7–8).

   3. Joppa is approximately thirty miles to the south of Caesarea. The men sent by Cornelius depart and, at around noon the following day, arrive in Joppa.

II. How did God reveal to Peter that the gospel was not just for Jews but also for Gentiles?

   A. We have to remember that Peter was still following the Jewish customs of the day.

     1. When Peter later met the messengers from Cornelius, he said, "It is against our law for a Jew to associate with or visit a Gentile" (Acts 10:28). There were many barriers for a Jew to associate with a Gentile—the Jew would be considered ritually unclean.

     2. The God of the Other Side came to break social barriers. Peter, in this moment, had to be willing to get past his prejudices and stereotypes and obey the Lord.

     3. The early believers thought they had to hold to all the Jewish ceremonies and rituals to be eligible for God's blessing. They did not understand the fullness of Jesus coming was a new covenant. They did not yet understand *grace* . . . but they soon would.

B. The transformation in Peter's thinking begins when God sends an unusual vision.

    1. Peter goes up on the roof to pray. He becomes hungry, and while the meal is being prepared in the house below, he falls into a trance (see verses 9–10).

    2. Peter has a vision in which heaven opens and a sheet—or some other kind of pure, clean, beautiful linen—is lowered down to the earth (see verse 11).

    3. Peter sees there are all kinds of four-footed animals, reptiles, and birds on top of this cloth. All of these animals were forbidden for him to consume (see verse 12).

C. Peter hears a voice that instructs him to get up, kill, and eat (see verse 13).

    1. Peter is mystified by this command. He has been told all of his life to *never* eat these kinds of animals. He tells God that he has never eaten anything unclean (see verse 14).

    2. God makes it very plain to Peter that this is an order. He tells Peter not to call anything impure that the Lord has made clean. This happens three times (see verses 15–16).

    3. We tend to ignore visions and dreams in our modern evangelical culture. But often—and still today—the Lord will speak to us through our dreams (see Job 33:14–15).

III. How did the vision that Peter received from God impact the history of the church?

A. The vision changes Peter's mindset about Gentiles in the church. Later, at the Jerusalem Council, he will join with Paul in arguing that the Gentiles do not need to become "Jewish" to follow Jesus (see Acts 15:6–11).

    1. Up until this moment, many of the Jews believed that the Messiah was coming for just the Jewish people. For many, there was no room for anyone unclean or ritually impure.

2. As Peter is pondering the meaning of the vision, he receives word the messengers sent by Cornelius have arrived at the house. The Holy Spirit tells Peter to meet them. Peter actually invites these Gentiles into the home as guests (see 10:17–23).

3. Peter travels with the group back to Caesarea. He meets Cornelius and tells him the message of salvation. Cornelius and his household receive Yeshua, Messiah Jesus, into their hearts and believe. They are baptized into the church (see verses 24–48).

B. Cornelius is the first Gentile convert mentioned in the Bible. Other Gentiles before him believed in Yahweh and worshiped him, but they are not recorded in Scripture.

1. The Gentiles known to follow Yahweh were called "God-fearers" (see Acts 10:2, 22; 13:26). They were viewed by the Jews of that day as second-class citizens.

2. There are parallels in the story of Cornelius and Peter that are relevant to us today. Both of these men started their journey of obedience to God by engaging in prayer.

3. These men had a posture of prayer. God heard their prayers and challenged them to reset their worldviews. We likewise have to be people of prayer.

C. The story of Cornelius and Peter encourages us to look at things through God's eyes.

1. When we intercede for others, we pray according to what we see in the natural. But God encourages us to open our spiritual eyes to see what the Holy Spirit is doing.

The Jerusalem Council

Peter's vision in Joppa, and subsequent realization that "God does not show favoritism but accepts from every nation the one who fears him and does what is right" (Acts 10:34–35), ignited a debate among the Jewish followers of Jesus that had likely been brewing for some time. As the gospel spread, more and more Gentiles were coming to the faith. The question for the Jewish believers was whether these believers needed to also adopt Jewish practices.

The matter came to a head when several Jewish believers from Jerusalem arrived in Syrian Antioch (where Paul and Silas were currently ministering) and began teaching that circumcision was necessary for salvation (see Acts 15:1). These individuals, known as "Judaizers," had preached a similar message among the Gentile congregations in Galatia. Paul and Barnabas soon fell into "sharp dispute and debate with them" (verse 2) and decided to go to Jerusalem to take the matter up with the apostles and James the Just, whom tradition states was the half-brother of Jesus and leader of the church in Jerusalem. It was determined that a council would be held among the elders of the church to resolve the matter.[32]

After much debate among the differing factions, Peter spoke to the council about the vision he had received at Joppa. "Brothers," he said, "you know that some time ago God made a choice among you that the Gentiles might hear from my lips the message of the gospel and believe. God, who knows the heart, showed that he accepted them by giving the Holy Spirit to them, just as he did to us. He did not discriminate between us and them, for he purified their hearts by faith. Now then, why do you try to test God by putting on the necks of Gentiles a yoke that neither we nor our ancestors have been able to bear? No! We believe it is through the grace of our Lord Jesus that we are saved, just as they are" (verses 7–11).

James the Just was known for scrupulously keeping to the Mosaic law, and the Judaizers likely expected that he would support their position. But after hearing from both sides, he determined, "It is my judgment, therefore, that we should not make it difficult for the Gentiles who are turning to God" (verse 19). In reaching this conclusion, James effectively swept aside the criticisms that had arisen about Paul and Silas' ministry to the Gentiles. The gospel would now be free to expand without such hindrances to "the ends of the earth" (1:8).[33]

2. Cornelius and Peter joined in God's plan. Cornelius could have denied that he had heard from the angel. Peter could have denied that the vision he received was from the Lord. But because they were men of prayer, they surrendered their will to God.

3. When we join with what God is doing, we embark on an incredible adventure. We learn to rely on his supernatural strength instead of our own natural strength.

IV. What do we learn from this story about going to the "other side" to reach people?

A. When we partner with God, we will be surprised at how powerfully he uses us.

1. When Peter went up on that roof in Joppa to pray, he had no idea that God was about to change the entire trajectory of the church and start reaching out to the Gentiles.

2. Peter's intimacy with God had taught him to trust completely in the Lord. Both Peter and Cornelius were used to living according to the customs their societies dictated. Yet suddenly, they had to consider a new way of seeing and of believing.

3. God will challenge us like he did with Peter and Cornelius. "In him we live and move and have our being" (Acts 17:28). He calls us to go to the "other side" each day.

B. The missional life that God intends us to be living requires us to see things in a new way.

   1. We need to train ourselves to look for God in the ordinary. Sometimes, we work so hard to find the next great missional endeavor that we forget the mission field that is right in front of us where we live.

   2. We raise money to go to great places where the gospel needs to be shared—and that is fantastic. But there are people right next door who also need a dose of godly love.

   3. We can be people who *welcome* outsiders into the church instead of people who *judge* them. This begins by loving them right where they are.

C. Only God has the right to judge (see James 4:12). Only Jesus decides who goes where.

   1. Jesus said, "I am the way and the truth and the life. No one comes to the Father except through me" (John 14:6). Some view this as intolerant, but it is actually good news.

   2. The one who loved us so much that he was willing to die for us on the cross is the one who is going to decide where we spend eternity.

   3. The story of Cornelius and Peter reveals that God loves a generous heart. The role we have been given, as followers of Jesus, is simply to love one another.

Discuss | 35 minutes

Take some time to discuss what you just watched by answering the following questions. There are some suggested questions below to help you begin your discussion, but feel free to pick any of the additional questions as time allows.

Suggested Questions

1. Ask someone in the group to read aloud Acts 10:1–8. Cornelius is described in this passage not only as a Roman centurion but also as a God-fearing man who prayed to Yahweh and gave generously to those in need. What did the angel who visited Cornelius instruct him to do? How did Cornelius respond to these instructions?

2. Ask someone to continue reading aloud Acts 10:9–23. The Lord had instructed his people in the old covenant about what kinds of animals he considered to be clean and unclean (see Leviticus 11). So it is little wonder that Peter was astonished when the voice told him to arise, kill, and eat these kinds of animals. What was God saying to Peter about the new covenant that had been enacted through Jesus?

3. Which of the two men do you resonate with the most—Cornelius, who was called to take a step of faith even though he wasn't a "man of faith"; or Peter, who was called to take a step of faith outside his religious walls, rules, and regulations? What are some of the reasons you can give as to why you resonate with that character?

4. Ask someone to read the conclusion to the story in Acts 10:23–48. What did Peter come to recognize about how God viewed the Jews and the Gentiles? What happened as a result of Peter's willingness to invite Cornelius' messengers into his house, travel back with them to Caesarea, and share the gospel with Cornelius and his family?

Additional Questions

5. The vision that God sent to Peter on that rooftop in Joppa challenged a system of beliefs that he had held ever since he was a child. When is a time that God did something astounding like this to change your view about something or someone?

6. Ask someone in the group to read Acts 15:1–11. In this story, a council is held in Jerusalem to determine whether Gentiles must be "circumcised" (accept Jewish practices) in order to be considered saved. How would Peter's experience with Cornelius have informed his decision on this matter (see verses 7–11)? How did this decision ultimately impact the church and how we operate as believers today?

7. Both Cornelius and Peter began their journey of obedience to God by engaging in prayer. What does this say about the importance of prayer in our lives?

8. Think about some of the divisions you see in the church today, whether it's between ethnicities, age groups, or people with different beliefs. How do you feel about these divisions? How does this study give you a hope and vision for this divisiveness?

Respond | 10 minutes

Review the outline for the video teaching and any notes you took. In the space below, write down your most significant takeaway from this session.

Pray | 10 minutes

End your time by praying together, thanking God for bringing both Jews and Gentiles into his family. Ask if anyone has any prayer requests to share. Write those requests down in the space below so you and your group members can pray about them in the week ahead.

Name   Request

Personal Study

As you discussed this week, the story of Cornelius and Peter represents a turning point for the early church, for it was the first time that Jewish followers of Jesus considered the fact that God would also accept Gentiles into the faith. The story touches on our own tendency to create divisions in the church, explains how to listen to God's call, and shows how the Lord can work through ordinary people and circumstances. As you explore these themes this week, be sure to write down your responses to the questions, as you will be given a few minutes to share your insights at the start of the next session if you are doing this study with others. If you are reading *The God of the Way* alongside this study, first review chapter 17 in the book.

-Day 1-

A New Way of Thinking

Have you ever tried to return to an old childhood home only to find it is not there anymore? Maybe it was knocked down and replaced by a modern townhome. Perhaps your entire street is now a shopping mall. Or maybe it is now the site of a warehouse or other industrial building. Whatever the cause, it is disorienting to know what was once there but not see it anymore.

This can happen with our faith. As we journey with God, we learn new things about him as we study the Bible and listen to the voice of the Holy Spirit speaking into our hearts. This can cause us to release certain beliefs along the way that we realize were not from God or based on his Word. Rather, they represent teachings that were passed down to us or we were told we should believe. This is an inevitable part of the Christian journey . . . as disorienting as it can be.

In the story told in Acts 10, we see Peter experience this after receiving a vision from the Lord and spending time with a Gentile named Cornelius. As a faithful Jewish man, Peter would have abided by the laws that determined what was acceptable to eat and what was not. He would have held to the Jewish practices of who was considered acceptable to spend time with and who was not. But this all got turned upside down for Peter. God was challenging him to let go of certain long-held beliefs that had not come from the Lord.

Peter was being educated in the new covenant in Christ. It was indeed good news, but that didn't mean it was easy for Peter to accept. It is hard to let go of beliefs that we have held our entire lives. It is challenging to enter a new way of thinking, seeing, and believing. But when we know this "new way" of thinking comes from God and is supported by Scripture, we can be confident it is the right way.

Our old "house" of belief may need to be renovated or come down altogether, but what is rebuilt will be even better than what was there before.

Read | Romans 12:1–2, Isaiah 26:3–4, and 2 Corinthians 3:12–18

Reflect

1. In Romans 12:1–2, the apostle Paul first urges followers of Jesus to offer themselves wholly to God as a "living sacrifice." What does he then say about the dangers of conforming to the world's way of thinking? What are believers to do instead?

2. According to Isaiah 26:3–4, how do we find God's perfect peace for our lives? What does it mean that the Lord is "the Rock eternal"?

3. In 2 Corinthians 3:12–18, Paul refers to the story of Moses coming down from Mount Sinai and having to cover his face because it was radiant with God's glory (see Exodus 34:29). How does Paul use this imagery to show how God gives revelation to people under the new covenant? What happens when we have "unveiled faces"?

4. What are some beliefs you held growing up that God has helped you to release? What did it feel like to let go of those beliefs?

Pray | Thank God today that he has "lifted the veil" so you can fully see his new covenant of which you are a part. Ask him to help you let go of any wrong beliefs that are keeping you from knowing him or experiencing his love. Ask him to give you the courage to let those beliefs go.

Day 2

A New Way of Acting

When Jesus was speaking to the crowds in the Sermon on the Mount, he made this startling statement: "Do not think that I have come to abolish the Law or the Prophets; I have not come to abolish them but to fulfill them" (Matthew 5:17). Jesus was actually saying that he was the *fulfillment* of the law and the prophecies that God had given to his people in the Old Testament. Everything under the old covenant pointed toward him in the new covenant.

God had intended his people to be a blessing to the nations (see Genesis 12:3), but he also called them to be holy or "set apart" (see Leviticus 11:44; 20:24). He did not want them to be influenced by the idolatrous practices of the nations around them. Over the centuries, this had developed into an "us" and "them" mentality. However, with the arrival of Jesus, all nations would be "grafted" into God's plan of salvation (see Romans 11:11–24).

As we have seen, this was a struggle for the early Jewish followers of Jesus to grasp. While it is tempting to categorize them as discriminatory or shortsighted, they were simply imposing the rules they had followed all of their lives under the old covenant. They were willing to accept the Gentiles into the faith, but they were going about it the wrong way.

As followers of Jesus, we've now had more than 2,000 years to evolve, grow, and develop in our way of thinking about God's grace. Yet we are still not experts. We fail to have grace for ourselves . . . and we fail to have grace for others. We easily slip into an old covenant mentality where we assume we become justified before God not through our faith in Jesus but through the works we do that we think will maintain our salvation (see Galatians 2:16).

Jesus ushered in not only a new way of thinking about God's grace for the world but also a new way of acting toward those we once considered to be on the "other side." Jesus levels the playing field. The good news is for everyone.

Read | Genesis 12:1–3, Genesis 17:10–14, and Acts 15:12–21

Reflect

1. In Genesis 12:1–3, we read how God called Abram (later renamed Abraham) to leave his country and go to a new homeland that the Lord would reveal to him. What blessing did God say he would bestow on Abram and his descendants if he obeyed?

2. According to Genesis 17:10–14, what was the significance of circumcision for the Jewish people? Why do you think the Jewish believers felt these rules should apply to the Gentiles who wanted to receive salvation and enter into the church?

3. James, the half-brother of Jesus, was the leader of the church in Jerusalem, where a council was held to determine whether Gentiles who came into the faith needed to be circumcised (and follow other Jewish practices). In Acts 15:16–18, he quotes the prophet Amos. What does this prophecy reveal about God's plan for the Gentiles?

4. What do you struggle with more—having grace for yourself or for others? What rules or rituals do you tend to attach to the free gift of God's grace?

Pray | Come before the Father in prayer. Thank him for the grace and mercy you have received through Jesus Christ. Ask him to help you accept grace for yourself and extend it to others.

- Day 3 -

Reluctant Evangelists

In the story for this week, Cornelius received a visit from an angel who instructed him to "send men to Joppa to bring back a man named Simon who is called Peter" (Acts 10:5). Joppa is today known as Jaffa and is a coastal city located approximately thirty miles south of Caesarea. The modern city of Tel Aviv, the largest metropolitan area in the nation of Israel, was founded on the outskirts of Jaffa in 1909 and today encompasses the ancient city.[34]

Hundreds of years before Peter was in that city, another follower of God spent time in Joppa: a prophet named Jonah. This is likely no coincidence, as Jonah's story parallels Peter's story in that both men were called by God to go to the Gentiles. In Jonah's case, this direction was to go to Ninevah, a city that was known for its wickedness (see Jonah 1:2). The prophet Jonah was instructed to warn them that God would destroy the city if they did not turn from their evil ways.

Jonah, if you are familiar with the story, did not obey God. Instead he headed for a place called Tarshish, which was about as far away as he could go from Nineveh. To get there, he caught a boat in the city of Joppa. God sent a storm to get him back on track, Jonah ended up in the sea and then in the belly of a giant fish, and then the fish spit him up on the land near Nineveh. From there, Jonah obeyed God and (reluctantly) spread the Lord's message to the people.

Jonah was a reluctant evangelist. Still, God used him, and the people believed and repented (see 3:5). You might think this would have changed Jonah's mind about the people of Nineveh—that he, like Peter, would have realized the Ninevites were part of God's divine plan. But the last chapter of Jonah does not suggest much change had occurred in the prophet.

How often do we behave like Jonah? How often do we stay in our communities instead of heed God's call to the "other side"? Like it or not, there is a bit of Jonah in us all.

Read | Jonah 4:1–11

Reflect

1. The events in this chapter occur after the Ninevites repent and God chooses to not send destruction against them (see 3:10). How does Jonah feel about Nineveh being spared—and why might he have felt this way? How does God respond to Jonah?

2. God provides Jonah with an interesting object lesson to show him where his concern for people should lie. What lesson does God teach Jonah through the leafy plant?

3. The Bible does not tell us how Jonah responded to God's final words. Why do you think that is—and do you think Jonah was changed by this experience?

4. When have you been a reluctant evangelist like Jonah? Who in your community might God be calling you to have compassion on and reach with his love?

Pray | Confess to God any reluctance you've had in the past about following his calling. Tell him about your fears, hesitations, and judgments. Ask him to protect you from having a heart like Jonah and to instead give you the compassion and mercy of Jesus.

- Day 4 -

Willing Evangelists

Unlike the prophet Jonah, both Peter and Cornelius were willing participants in God's work of bringing the Jews and Gentiles into the church. This was because, as you learned in this week's group time, they were poised and ready to participate in what God was already doing. Peter and Cornelius shared four key traits that allowed them to be ready in this way.

First, they were prayerful. Cornelius is described as a man who "prayed to God regularly" (Acts 10:2). Peter went up on the roof at noontime to pray (see verse 9), which indicates he also had a regular habit of prayer. Both men were primed to hear God's voice.

Second, they were God-fearing. Cornelius is described as "God-fearing" (verse 2) even though he was not yet a follower of Jesus. The word *fear* here does not mean that he was afraid of God but rather that he was in awe of God. Peter also certainly revered God, which means that both men were willing to do what the Lord asked when the time came.

Third, they were hospitable. Cornelius is described as a generous man who gave to those in need, and he welcomed Peter to his home (see verses 2, 24–25). Peter welcomed Cornelius' men into his home (see verse 23). Hospitality is necessary to reach others with the gospel.

Fourth, they were willing to partner with God. Peter and Cornelius did not do things their own way. Rather, they joined in the work that God was already doing. They were partners with God and allowed him to guide them to help fulfill his plan for the Gentiles.

Prayerful, God-fearing, hospitable, and willing to partner—these are essential qualities for the willing evangelist. When we are already poised to do God's work, he can use us to further his kingdom. When our eyes, ears, and hearts are already tuned to him, we will be quick to respond, quick to partner, and quick to help. On the other hand, when we are not regularly doing these things, it will be harder for us to hear God's voice. May we be poised as Peter and Cornelius were—ready to respond to God's call at any moment.

Read | 2 Timothy 4:1–5 and Acts 10:44–48

Reflect

1. The book of 2 Timothy was penned by Paul to a fellow disciple and coworker in the faith named Timothy. When does Paul say Timothy should be prepared to speak the Word? How can Timothy remain in a state of "perpetual preparedness"?

2. How did Peter and Cornelius embody Paul's instructions in Acts 10:44–48? What happened as a result of Peter and Cornelius' willingness to partner with God?

3. Who do you know who exhibits attributes of being prayerful, God-fearing, hospitable, and willing to partner with God? What spiritual fruit do you see in that person's life?

4. What spiritual practices do you feel might be lacking in your life? How could doing these practices keep you in a state of being more prepared to follow God's call?

Pray | Begin your prayer time in silence and just spend a few minutes listening for God's voice. Is your heart and spirit poised and ready to listen, or are you distracted by other things? Notice any of these distractions that arise, and ask God to help attune your heart to his voice.

-Day 5-

Visions and Wonders

Peter and Cornelius' stories started with a vision. Cornelius had a vision of an angel of the Lord who instructed him to send men to Peter. Peter had a vision of unclean animals that God declared to be clean. These visions were not the end of their stories but just the beginning. Peter and Cornelius responded to them, contemplating their meaning and doing what they were told.

Maybe you have never been visited by an angel or fallen into a trance as Peter did, but God has still given you a vision. Visions are what allow you to imagine what isn't already there. They can be as simple as seeing yourself going to a certain college, having a certain job, imagining your children having a happy future, or imagining your church thriving.

Having a vision for your life is crucial. As we read in Proverbs 29:18, "Where there is no vision, the people perish" (KJV). Peter and Cornelius' vision allowed them to have a new dream for the Gentiles and the Christian faith—one in which everyone was included, everyone belonged, and everyone was considered "clean." This was something Peter had likely not been able to imagine before. He had no vision for the Gentiles until God gave him one. Once he saw the vision, he was able to pursue it and see it come to fruition at Cornelius' home.

Of course, our visions do not always come to fruition so easily. They can take time to develop. They can pan out differently than we imagined. They can be better than we imagined! When our vision is from God, we can be confident he will complete it and likely surprise us in the process.

Perhaps you feel discouraged in your vision. Like Peter, you have a vision for the church—something you have been praying and hoping God will do—but that vision hasn't yet come to fruition. *Know that it may not in your lifetime.* Visions are on God's timeline. But you can trust his timing is perfect. In the meantime, keep working toward what you cannot see today. Know that with God, all things are possible (see Matthew 19:26).

Read | Jeremiah 29:10–14 and Habakkuk 2:2–3

Reflect

1. Jeremiah and Habakkuk are believed to have been prophets to the nation of Judah shortly before and during the time of the Babylonian capture of Jerusalem. They brought the word of God to the people of Judah and gave them a glimpse of what was to come. What kind of vision did Jeremiah present to God's people?

2. What did God say about Habakkuk's vision and the timing of it?

3. What visions has God given you, whether they are for your personal, vocational, relational, or spiritual life? How do you know these visions are from God?

4. What do these passages say about the nature and timing of the visions God has given you? How could you find encouragement for your visions from these passages?

Pray | Ask God to restore his vision to you today. If you have forgotten it, gotten off track, or lost faith in it, ask him to remind you of what he wants for you—a hope and a future.

For Next Week

Before you meet again with your group next week, read chapter 18 and the Conclusion in *The God of the Way*. Also go back and complete any of the study and reflection questions from this personal study that you weren't able to finish.

Schedule

WEEK 6

BEFORE GROUP MEETING	Read chapter 18 in *The God of the Way* Read the Welcome section (page 133)
GROUP MEETING	Discuss the Connect questions Watch the video teaching for session 6 Discuss the questions that follow as a group Do the closing exercise and pray (pages 133–144)
PERSONAL STUDY – DAY 1	Complete the daily study (pages 146–147)
PERSONAL STUDY – DAY 2	Complete the daily study (pages 148–149)
PERSONAL STUDY – DAY 3	Complete the daily study (pages 150–151)
PERSONAL STUDY – DAY 4	Complete the daily study (pages 152–153)
PERSONAL WRAP-UP	Complete the daily study (pages 154–155) Connect with your group about the next study that you want to go through together

The Power of Unity

WE ARE STRONGER TOGETHER

How good and pleasant it is when God's people live together in unity! It is like precious oil poured on the head, running down on the beard, running down on Aaron's beard, down on the collar of his robe. It is as if the dew of Hermon were falling on Mount Zion. For there the LORD bestows his blessing, even life forevermore.

PSALM 133:1–3

Welcome | Read On Your Own

Throughout this study, you have explored how the Lord actively seeks and saves those who are on the "other side." You first studied how Jesus went to the other side of the Sea of Galilee to heal a demon-possessed man. You saw how he went out of his way to reach a Samaritan Woman and told a story of two sons who lived very different lives but were accepted by the same father. In the last session, you discussed how God told Peter the gospel was for Jews and Gentiles alike.

These stories reveal that God considers those who put their faith in his Son to be members of his own family. Paul wrote, "There is neither Jew nor Gentile, neither slave nor free, nor is there male and female, for you are all one in Christ Jesus" (Galatians 3:28). As members of God's family, we are called to be united and join together for a common purpose. Our faith in Jesus was never meant to be a solitary practice. Rather, we were meant to gain strength and encouragement from our fellow brothers and sisters in Jesus.

In this session, we will look at how a paralyzed man benefited from the unity of his four friends. These men were so determined to bring their friend to Jesus—so filled with faith the Messiah could heal him—that they went to extreme measures to make it happen. The actions of these men actually made a demand on Jesus' power. The paralyzed man was healed not necessarily because of his own faith but because of the faith of his friends!

In a world full of division, we cannot forget that Jesus has called us to be one. Not to be separated or to go it alone . . . but to be in it together for the sake of the gospel. And when we do join together in this way, we will be amazed at how God will move in our midst.

Connect | 15 minutes

Welcome to session 6 of *The God of the Other Side*. To get things started for this week's final group time, discuss one of the following questions:

- What is a key insight or takeaway from last week's personal study that you would like to share with the group?

— or —

- Where do you see the most division in the world today? Where do you see the most division among believers in the church today?

Watch | 20 minutes

Now watch the video for this session. As you watch, use the following outline to record any thoughts or concepts that stand out to you.

I. How does the story of the four friends demonstrate the power of unity?

A. The four friends of the paralyzed man in Mark 2:1–5 represent those kinds of people in our lives who have faith for us even when we may not have faith enough for ourselves.

1. Paul tells us to "run in such a way as to get the prize" (1 Corinthians 9:24). But we all need to run together in unity so we can break down every barrier against us.

2. God has asked his bride—the fellowship of brothers and sisters in Jesus—to unify at all costs. We are to be "united in mind and thought" (1:10).

3. We see the power of unity at work in the story of the four men who brought their friend to see Jesus when he was in Capernaum. When the people learned Jesus was there, they gathered in such numbers that the house was packed (see Mark 2:1–2).

B. Everyone was talking about Jesus and the miracles that he was doing in the region. The power of that testimony caused the faith in these four men to rise up.

1. We do not know if these men had witnessed Jesus' miracles. But we do know they had a friend they cared about who was completely paralyzed.

2. The men decide to bring their friend to Jesus to see if he can heal him. They come to the house where Jesus is staying but can find no way to get inside (see verse 3).

Homes in First-Century Galilee

The typical dwelling in first-century Israel was neither large nor grand. Most of the people at that time lived in the countryside and built modest homes in small villages that were scattered about wherever the presence of water could be found. In the arid regions of the country, houses were more concentrated around the few springs and wells that existed. Apart from Jerusalem and four to five other locations, all the towns in ancient Israel were quite small.[35]

Archaeological excavations have revealed that the typical home in Galilee was built of basalt (a dark volcanic rock) and was comprised of one to two stories. Stonemasons used wooden scaffolds to set the larger rocks of the walls and wedged smaller stones in between to provide stability for the structure. Sometimes, the walls were plastered with mud and straw. The doorframe was built of shaped stones and covered by a wooden door. The roof was typically made of wooden beams covered with tree branches or thatch and then covered with clay. The clay served to absorb the water when it rained and kept it from dripping down inside.

Kitchens in first-century homes typically included a domed oven used for heating and cooking. Family members who prepared the meals used animal dung, the pulp of pressed olives, or small branches for fuel. Hand grinders for making flour, cooking pots, stone water jars, and baskets for storing food were all employed in the kitchen. Homes might have a small garden, vineyards with grapes and olive trees, and livestock out back for food. There was also usually a larger family room where eating, storing food, and socializing took place. The inhabitants slept on wooden-frame beds with ropes stretched over them. A mat was placed across the ropes, and sometimes more than one family member slept in the same bed.

A storeroom housed the important farming tools and supplies the family needed to survive. This was generally a wooden plow, a sickle, brooms, a winnowing fork, a sieve for grain, rope made from plant fibers, and an animal skin used as a churn for butter or cheese. When the harvest was ready, family members would cut the grain with a sickle and place it on a stone surface called a "threshing floor." There it was crushed by a small sled dragged by animals, and then the mixture was tossed into the air. The lighter straw and chaff would blow away, while the heavier grain would fall to the stone floor where it could be collected.[36]

3. The villages in the region of Galilee (like Capernaum) were not large and could easily get overcrowded if the people from the countryside flooded into them.

C. So the men find themselves standing outside the home, looking in through the windows. We can visualize just how stuffy and packed it was—there was absolutely no room to get another body inside.

1. But the friends quickly come up with an ingenious way to reach Jesus. They make their way up to the roof of the home and begin to create an opening (see verse 4).

2. The roof would have been made of thatch that could be removed layer by layer. The material would have rained down on the people inside as the men dug it away.

3. We do not know how the owner of the home reacted when he saw his roof being destroyed. He was likely not happy at the destruction and mess he was witnessing!

II. How does Jesus respond to the faith of the four men who lowered down their friend?

A. The four friends had both faith in Jesus and the tenacity to put their plan into action. What is not as clear is what level of faith the paralyzed man himself had in Jesus.

1. The friends had faith enough for him. The same is often true in our lives—there are times when we get discouraged and lose hope. We need friends who believe for us.

2. The faith of the four friends demonstrates the power of unity. When people believe for us and take action on our behalf, it builds up our own faith in the Lord.

3. Jesus, presumably, would have been standing in the middle of the mess as the thatched roof came down. The people around him would have been getting irritated. Jesus could have reacted many different ways . . . but he always saw the need of the person first.

B. We can picture Jesus calming everyone down as the men started to remove the roof. He knew God was in this moment. He might have even tried to make some room.

1. Most of us would have been worried about the mess and cleanup required to repair the roof. But God's thoughts and ways are above our own (see Isaiah 55:8).

2. What drove Jesus in this story—and in every story found in the Bible—is *love*. He said, "Love one another. As I have loved you, so you must love one another" (John 13:34).

3. Jesus saw the faith of the four friends and, out of love for the paralyzed man, said to him, "Son, your sins are forgiven" (Mark 2:5).

C. This statement caused the teachers of the law, who were watching Jesus, to erupt. They accused him of blasphemy, for only God could forgive sins (see verses 6–7).

    1. Jesus immediately knew in his spirit what they were thinking. He paid no attention to their criticism but turned his attention back to the paralyzed man (see verses 8–11).

    2. The four friends also did not heed the religious leaders. They were unified and focused on bringing the one they cared about before the one whom they had heard could heal him.

    3. The collective faith of the men made a demand on Jesus' power. These men's faith *and* their action in getting their friend before Jesus brought forth the power of God.

III. What does God say about the anointing we receive when we dwell in unity?

    A. The collective faith of the four men became a catalyst that released God's anointing. We read what can happen when believers join together in unity in Psalm 133.

      1. The psalmist declares that it is "good and pleasant" when brothers and sisters join together in unity. It brings about God's anointing (see verses 1–2).

      2. The psalmist depicts Aaron, the high priest, being anointed with oil. The oil is poured over his head and drips down his beard, to his robe, and to the hem of his garment.

Unity in Paul's Letters

The four men who brought their paralyzed friend to Jesus collectively had faith. They had a bond of unity, and when Jesus saw their combined faith, it released God's anointing for the healing of the paralyzed man. Unity in the family of God is critical. It was so important to Paul that he frequently commanded his congregations to put aside differences and join together as one.

Corinth. The believers in Corinth were dividing into factions as a result of their loyalties to different leaders and teachers. Some were evidently spouting slogans such as, "I follow Paul," "I follow Apollos," "I follow Peter," or even, "I follow Christ" (see 1 Corinthians 1:12). This last party might have adopted a "no creed but Christ" approach in an attempt to not have to claim allegiance to any human leader. Paul's counsel was for them to put these petty differences aside. "I appeal to you, brothers and sisters, in the name of our Lord Jesus Christ, that all of you agree with one another in what you say and that there be no divisions among you, but that you be perfectly united in mind and thought" (verse 10).[37]

Ephesus. The church in Ephesus, like most of Paul's congregations, was comprised of a diverse mix of Jews and Gentiles from different backgrounds and walks of life. They were also experiencing some level of persecution for their beliefs. Paul instructed them to bear with each other and "make every effort to keep the unity of the Spirit through the bond of peace" (Ephesians 4:3). Paul did not view their unity as an option or a luxury. Rather, the believers were to consciously and continuously pursue the unity that the Holy Spirit brings.[38]

Galatia. The divisions taking place in Paul's churches in Galatia were less a matter of internal strife and more a result of outside influences. Evidently, teachers had arrived in the region who were proclaiming a different gospel than the one Paul had preached—a gospel centered on doing works to attain salvation rather than relying solely on the grace of God. Paul reminded these believers that before they came to faith in Jesus, they "were held in custody under the law" (Galatians 3:23). But now, they were "children of God through faith" (verse 26). As such, they had to remain united, for "there is neither Jew nor Gentile, neither slave nor free, nor is there male and female, for you are all one in Christ Jesus" (verse 28).[39]

3. The anointing that comes through unity is abundant and overflowing. It is like the morning dew—the fresh dew—that falls on Mount Hermon (see verse 3).

B. The psalmist concludes, "There the LORD bestows his blessing, even life forevermore" (verse 3). This is one of the richest promises for the bride of Christ.

1. If we link arms and unify—trusting each other and forgiving one another—it releases an anointing that comes through the body of Christ into an unbelieving world.

2. We see this portrayed in Micah 5:7: "The purged and select company of Jacob will be like an island in the sea of peoples. They'll be like dew from GOD, like summer showers not mentioned in the weather forecast, not subject to calculation or control" (MSG).

3. Jesus also said in John 17:20–21: "I pray also for those who will believe in me through their message, that all of them may be one, Father, just as you are in me and I am in you. May they also be in us so that the world may believe that you have sent me."

C. The unity of the four men and their faith released the anointing of God over their paralyzed friend. The man's sins were forgiven and he was healed (see Mark 2:12).

1. The man went from being paralyzed to walking. In the same way, when believers unify, the world will go from being paralyzed to running in the freedom of Jesus.

2. We are seeing many moves of God in our world today where he is making his presence known. Jesus said, "For where two or three gather in my name, there am I with them" (Matthew 18:20).

3. God is waiting for the invitation to make his presence known (see James 5:14–16).

IV. What is the challenge for believers today in reaching those on the "other side"?

1. We need to stop viewing the church as a set of buildings. The Greek word for church, *ekklesia*, refers not to a structure but to a gathering of people—a movement.

2. We need to seek to understand the context in which the Bible was written and study it rabbinically. This does not mean that we learn Hebrew and Greek, but that we study translations faithful to the original and allow ourselves to be guided by the Holy Spirit.

3. When we love others as Jesus instructed us to love them, it prompts us to move out of our comfort zones to share that love with those on the "other side."

4. Our lives will never be dull if we choose to follow Jesus to the other side. The road to experiencing God's glory is the road to following Jesus wherever he leads.

Discuss | 35 minutes

Take some time to discuss what you just watched by answering the following questions. There are some suggested questions below to help you begin your discussion, but feel free to pick any of the additional questions as time allows.

Suggested Questions

1. Ask someone in the group to read aloud Mark 2:1–12. The four men who carried the paralyzed man had faith in Jesus' power to heal but also had a problem. There was no way for them to get their friend in front of Jesus because of the packed house. How did they resolve this problem? What did Jesus say when he saw their actions?

2. Sitting among the onlookers who had come to see Jesus were Pharisees or "teachers of the law" (verse 6). How did they react when Jesus said that the paralyzed man's sins were forgiven? Why do you think they responded in this way?

3. The teachers of the law were attempting to create division. How did Jesus silence them? What was Jesus revealing about his power and authority on earth?

4. In the end, the faith of the four friends made a demand on Jesus' power—their faith compelled the Lord to act on behalf of the paralyzed man. What does this story say about the power of unity? What can we expect God to do when we are united in faith?

Additional Questions

5. Ask someone to read aloud Psalm 133. What is the significance of oil in this passage? How is unity among believers linked to God's anointing in this psalm?

6. The prophet Micah wrote, "The purged and select company of Jacob will be like an island in the sea of peoples. They'll be like dew from GOD, like summer showers not mentioned in the weather forecast, not subject to calculation or control" (5:7 MSG). How does this passage parallel Psalm 133? What does this verse in Micah tell us about how others will see and experience the people of God when we are unified?

7. Have you ever witnessed a revival like the one mentioned in the teaching? If so, what was that experience like? How did you sense the anointing of God in that place?

8. How does your community need to experience revival and anointing from God? How could unity play a role in this? How could *you* play a role in bringing that unity?

Respond | 10 minutes

Review the outline for the video teaching and any notes you took. In the space below, write down your most significant takeaway from this session.

Pray | 10 minutes

End your time by praying together, thanking God for joining us together in his amazing and diverse family. Ask if anyone has any prayer requests to share. Write those requests down in the space below so you and your group members can pray about them in the week ahead.

Name   Request

Personal Study

As you have seen throughout this study, we serve a God who challenges us each and every day to go to the "other side" and reach those whom the world has deemed unreachable. We accomplish this mission not in our own strength but by joining with our fellow brothers and sisters in God's amazing family. When we join together in unity, we can expect God to move mightily in our midst, just as he did for the four friends who carried their paralyzed friend to Jesus. As you continue to explore these themes in this week's final personal study, be sure to write down your answers to the questions in the spaces provided. If you are reading *The God of the Way* alongside this study, first review chapter 18 and the Conclusion in the book.

—Day 1—

Power in Numbers

Even when we need it the most, it can be difficult for us to ask for help. It many ways, it can feel as if we are admitting weakness or defeat and giving up the independence in which we take so much pride. But those of us who have ever tried to accomplish a big task alone and then—*finally*—recruited help from friends and family know what a relief that help can be. We understand how much more we can get accomplished with others rather than on our own.

In the story you read this week, the paralyzed man had no choice but to ask for help. In a parallel account told in the Gospel of Luke, we read that people had come to see Jesus "from every village of Galilee and from Judea and Jerusalem" (5:17). The small town of Capernaum was bursting at the seams. It would likely have been difficult for the paralyzed man to get through the streets because of the crowds, much less into the home where Jesus was staying.

The man simply could not have gotten close enough to Jesus without his friends carrying him there. He could not have gotten right in front of Jesus if his friends hadn't then cut a hole in the roof and lowered him down. It is also apparent their faith had an impact on Jesus. These four friends cared for their friend, had faith that Jesus could heal the man, and did what was necessary to give him a chance at healing. The paralyzed man needed the tangible help of friends who cared about him and advocated on his behalf to Jesus.

Healing often happens this way within a body of believers . . . when others pray for us, help us, and carry us. We can pray for healing and have hope for healing, but it is when others join us in that prayer and hope that amazing things start to happen. So if you need physical, emotional, or spiritual healing, remember there is power in numbers. You don't have to go it alone. Invite others to join you, and see the healing power that unity in Jesus can bring.

Read | Ecclesiastes 4:9–12, James 5:13–16, and Galatians 6:1–2

Reflect

1. The author of Ecclesiastes 4:9–12 provides an eloquent assessment of why "two are better than one." What does he say are the benefits of having a good friend in life?

2. Both James and Paul state that the church has a role to play in physical and spiritual healing. According to James 5:13–16 and Galatians 6:1–2, what is that role?

3. When have you experienced or witnessed healing in the presence of community? How did this have an impact on your faith and trust in God?

4. What do you need healing for today? How could you invite friends, family, or mentors into this healing process?

Pray | Thank God for the healing power that he has over your life. Ask him to guide you to friends, family, and other members of your community who can help you heal today. Ask him to give you the courage to not suffer alone but to seek help from his body of believers.

-Day 2-

As We Are One

Think about that person in life with whom you share the closest connection. Perhaps it is a spouse, a parent, or a friend—someone who knows you well and knows you intimately. While the relationship you have with this person is certainly close, it is merely a glimpse into the relationship that Jesus has with God the Father. That relationship is one of complete unity and "oneness." It is a type of connection that is difficult for us to articulate or understand, yet it is a connection in which we all have been invited to join.

This is an incredible invitation. In the history of the world, the deities of other religions were typically pictured as being distant from people. In many cases, they acted out of their own petty ambitions, not caring about the impact that had on humans. But our God—the only *true* God—wants to be with us. He desired to be so near to us that he sent his Son and then his Spirit to dwell inside of us. God is not distant. He wants to be our most intimate relationship.

But the unity doesn't stop there. His vision for his people is that all would be one, united by Jesus, connected by the invisible thread that is the love, grace, and forgiveness of God. In a world full of division, name-calling, and conflict, Christians are to be unified by their common bond with God the Father, Jesus, and the Holy Spirit, and live in unity with each other.

When Jesus prayed in the Gospel of John for his disciples and for all believers, he had one primary request from the Father: that we would be unified. Unity was important to Jesus. In fact, it was of the utmost importance. So as you read parts of his prayer today, imagine Jesus picturing you when he asked this of the Father. He wants you to feel one with him and with your fellow believers. He does not expect you to walk the road of faith alone but to feel his presence and the presence of fellow Jesus-followers every step of the way.

Read | John 1:1–5 and John 17:20–23

Reflect

1. According to John 1:1–5, what was the relationship between God and the Word (Jesus)?

2. According to Jesus' prayer in John 17:20–23, why did he ask the Father that all believers would be as one? How did Jesus make this unity possible?

3. Why do you think unity among believers helps others to see and know God? How have you witnessed this type of unity at your church (or other faith community)?

4. Jesus prayed that his followers would reflect the unity of heart, mind, and purpose that he had with the Father. Do you feel one with other believers? Why or why not?

Pray | Spend some time before the Father in prayer. Ask him to show you how you could be unified with him and with Jesus. Ask him to show you how you could be more unified with the believers around you. Thank him for sending his Son, Jesus, so that we might all be one in him.

– Day 3 –

Faith, Unity, and Anointing

Look at any city in America today, and chances are that it was built with steel from Bethlehem Steel. For more than a century, this titan of industry based in Bethlehem, Pennsylvania, provided the steel that kept the nation growing. Bethlehem Steel was used in the construction of the Empire State Building, Hoover Dam, Golden Gate Bridge, and even the prison of Alcatraz.

However, by 2001 the company had filed for bankruptcy. Foreign competition had made it cheaper for companies to import steel. So the blast furnaces of Bethlehem Steel closed, taking most of the city's hopes with it. But in the decades that followed, the city experienced a revival. The local government decided to preserve the old steel plant and convert it into the backdrop for one of the most visually arresting art spaces in America. The city created the "SteelStacks" art campus—a ten-acre site filled with art, sculpture, music, and festivals.[40]

We don't often think of a revival in this way, but the term simply refers to an "improvement in the condition or strength of something." A revival can happen when people join together in unity and decide to not allow something to die. In the case of Bethlehem, this was a conscious decision to not allow the city to die. In our lives, it means a conscious decision to join with our fellow brothers and sisters in Jesus to pray for God to bring new life.

Perhaps you have witnessed this kind of revival. You know what it feels like to be in the presence of God, while in the presence of other believers, and together feel the Holy Spirit move in your midst. Or maybe you have heard of revivals like this taking place in the past, transforming cities and nations for the gospel. Faith, unity, and anointing . . . they all go together and in that order. When people of faith join together in unity, the anointing of the Holy Spirit will fall over them. So may our prayer today be the one that the psalmist prayed so long ago: "Revive us again, that your people may rejoice in you" (Psalm 85:6).

Read | Acts 1:12–14 and Acts 2:1–21

Reflect

1. Jesus had instructed his followers to remain in Jerusalem and wait for the baptism of the Holy Spirit (see Acts 1:4–5). How did the disciples and apostles respond to this command? What were they doing as they all gathered together (see verses 12–14)?

2. When the Day of Pentecost came, these believers were together in one place (see 2:1). They were all filled with the Holy Spirit and began to speak in other tongues, which caused confusion among those who overheard them. How did Peter explain what was happening? What had the prophet Joel said the Spirit would do (see verses 17–21)?

3. Why do you think the Spirit moves in this way when believers gather together?

4. When have you experienced the power of the Holy Spirit move like this while you were gathered together with other believers? What did the Spirit do?

Pray | Where do you want to see revival in your city, church, or community? Ask God to make it happen. Believe that he can and he will. Ask him what your role can be in inviting the Holy Spirit into that place.

— Day 4 —

Discord and Harmony

It is far easier to talk about unity than to actually live it out. This is especially true in today's culture, where people are becoming more and more divided religiously, politically, and morally. We don't want to be *associated* with those who think or believe differently than we do, much less be unified with them. But being unified does not necessarily mean we have to be the same.

According to the *Merriam-Webster Dictionary*, one definition of the word *unity* is "a condition of harmony: accord."[41] In music, harmony is made up of many parts. You can still hear each part in a piece of music, but it comes together to form something even more beautiful and powerful than a single melody. This is what unity can look like (and sound like) in the church. Multiple voices come together to form something that is better and stronger.

Unfortunately, it seems as if many of us today have lost the ability to harmonize. We want to keep all the sopranos separated off in one place and the altos and tenors separated out into their own places. We don't want to mix. This is not what Jesus ever intended for the church. He did not want us to all be the same—after all, he did invite Gentiles into the mix, and they sang a very different tune from the Jewish believers. Yet we have to remember these words from Paul: "Here there is no Gentile or Jew, circumcised or uncircumcised, barbarian, Scythian, slave or free, but Christ is all, and is in all" (Colossians 3:11).

Most likely, those who witnessed the great revivals of the past were not all of the same mind, ideologies, or denominations. Yet when they gathered together, the anointing of the Spirit fell and they were united by their love of God. This is what happens when we see beyond our differences and center on Jesus. We are unified in a way that brings God's anointing on us, and then we can be sent to share the good news, empowered by the presence of the Holy Spirit.

Read | Psalm 133:1–3

Reflect

1. Oil was used in ancient Israel as a sign of election or an endowment of the Holy Spirit.[42] Aaron was a high priest who would have been anointed with oil in this way. Hermon was a mountain in Israel with streams that flowed from it, so it would have had plenty of dew in the morning.[43] Given this, why do you think the psalmist compared the unity of God's people to anointing oil and the dew of Mount Hermon?

2. According to verse 3, what is the promise for believers who join together in unity?

3. Think about a symphony and all of the different instruments that play their part to contribute to the whole. How does this relate to the church? Why is it important for each person to play their own "part" but still contribute to the whole?

4. What steps will you take today to focus more on the similarities that you have with those in the church than on your individual differences?

Pray | Ask God to search your heart. Where are you focusing too much on differences when you could be focusing on Jesus? Where do you need to reach across the aisle in the name of unity? Ask God to give you the courage and love to truly unify with other believers.

— Day 5 —

Going Together to the Other Side

When Jesus instructed the disciples to go to the other side of the Sea of Galilee, he did not tell them to go there alone. Rather, we read that "Jesus made *the disciples* get into the boat" (Matthew 14:22, emphasis added). They were all to make the journey to the Decapolis together. We can only imagine what would have happened if each disciple had set off in his own boat and attempted to weather the storm that was about to arrive.

When God calls us to the other side, rarely does he expect or want us to go alone. Think about this in your own church. Your congregation likely supports missionaries around the world. How many of those missionaries are ministering alone? Hopefully none of them! Going to the other side is scary enough. Going alone can feel impossible.

Fortunately, the church is not a body made up of one believer but is made up of many believers. And the church is not meant to be a static entity, confined to a building, but to be a movement in the world. As discussed in this week's group time, the Greek word translated as *church* is *ekklesia*, which is made up of two words: *ek*, which means "out"; and *kaleo*, which means "to call."[44]

The church is the place where we are called to go out into the world. We are not called to remain static or stuck in the same stagnant position. No, the church is a place of movement where believers spread the good news. Alone, this is difficult to do, but together with fellow believers, we are emboldened, empowered, and have the anointing of the Holy Spirit.

You may question your ability to go and serve those on the other side. Maybe you don't have the gift of evangelism, prophecy, or preaching. But this is the beauty of unity in the church! Someone else will have those gifts, freeing you to give of the gifts that you do possess. Whatever those are, your gifts in the context of the church—a body of believers—are valuable and needed. Wherever you go in your calling, you don't have to go it alone.

Read | Romans 12:6–8, Ephesians 4:11–13, Acts 6:1–4

Reflect

1. Paul says that "we have different gifts, according to the grace given to each of us" (Romans 12:6). Which (if any) of the gifts that he lists in this passage do you think you have? How could you use this gift to reach those on the "other side"?

2. What are some of the different roles in the church that Paul lists in Ephesians 4:11–13? Why is it important for the church to have these different kinds of roles?

3. In Acts 6:1–4, we see how the church benefits as a whole when believers decide to share the tasks in unity. What issue was brought to the disciples? What choice did the disciples make in regard to focusing on what they felt were their primary roles?

4. Remember that the church is the *ekklesia*—a "calling out" of followers of Jesus into the world. As you have gone through this study, what represents the "other side" to which you believe God is calling you? Who can join with you in that mission?

Pray | As you close out your time in this study, thank God for all that he has taught you. Thank him for the knowledge and the wisdom that you have gained by studying the Bible—the Word of God. Ask him to keep working in you as you take these lessons and cross to the other side.

Leader's Guide

Thank you for your willingness to lead your group through this study! What you have chosen to do is valuable and will make a great difference in the lives of others. *The God of the Other Side* is a six-session Bible study built around video content and small-group interaction. As the group leader, imagine yourself as the host of a party. Your job is to take care of your guests by managing the details so that when your guests arrive, they can focus on one another and on the interaction around the topic for that session.

Your role as the group leader is not to answer all the questions or reteach the content—the video, book, and study guide will do most of that work. Your job is to guide the experience and cultivate your small group into a connected and engaged community. This will make it a place for members to process, question, and reflect—not necessarily receive more instruction.

There are several elements in this leader's guide that will help you as you structure your study and reflection time, so be sure to follow along and take advantage of each one.

Before You Begin

Before your first meeting, make sure the group members have a copy of this study guide. Alternatively, you can hand out the study guides at your first meeting and give the members some time to look over the material and ask any preliminary questions. Also make sure they are aware that they have access to the streaming videos at any time by following the instructions provided. During your first meeting, ask the members to provide their name, phone number, and email address so you can keep in touch with them.

Generally, the ideal size for a group is eight to ten people, which will ensure that everyone has enough time to participate in discussions. If you have more people, you might want to break up the main group into smaller subgroups. Encourage those who show up at the first meeting to commit to attending the duration of the study, as this will help the group members get to know one another, create stability for the group, and help you know how to best prepare to lead them through the material.

Each of the sessions begins with an opening reflection in the "Welcome" section. The questions that follow in the "Connect" section serve as an icebreaker to get the group members thinking about the topic. Some people may want to tell a long story in response to one of these questions, but the goal is to keep the answers brief. Ideally, you want everyone in the group to get a chance to answer, so try to keep the responses to a minute or less. If you have talkative group members, say up front that everyone needs to limit their answer to one minute.

Give the group members a chance to answer, but also tell them to feel free to pass if they wish. With the rest of the study, it's generally not a good idea to have everyone answer every question—a free-flowing discussion is more desirable. But with the opening icebreaker questions, you can go around the circle. Encourage shy people to share, but don't force them.

At your first meeting, let the members know each session contains a personal study section they can use to continue to engage with the content until the next meeting. While this is optional, it will help them cement the concepts presented during the group study time and help them better understand the character, nature, and attributes of the God of the Other Side. Let them know that if they choose to do so, they can watch the video for the next session by accessing the streaming code. Invite them to bring any questions and insights to your next meeting, especially if they had a breakthrough moment or didn't understand something.

Preparation for Each Session

As the leader, there are a few things you should do to prepare for each meeting:

- **Read through the session.** This will help you become more familiar with the content and know how to structure the discussion times.

- **Decide how the videos will be used.** Determine whether you want the members to watch the videos ahead of time (again, via the streaming access code provided with this guide) or together as a group.

- **Decide which questions you want to discuss.** Based on the length of your group discussions, you may not be able to get through all the questions. So look over the recommendations for the suggested and additional questions in each session and choose which ones you definitely want to cover.

- **Be familiar with the questions you want to discuss.** When the group meets, you'll be watching the clock, so make sure you are familiar with the questions that you have selected. In this way, you will ensure that you have the material more deeply in your mind than your group members.

- **Pray for your group.** Pray for your group members and ask God to lead them as they study his Word.

In many cases, there will be no one "right" answer to the question. Answers will vary, especially when the group members are being asked to share their personal experiences.

Structuring the Discussion Time

You will need to determine with your group how long you want to meet so you can plan your time accordingly. Suggested times for each section have been provided in this study guide, and if you adhere to these times, your group will meet for ninety minutes, as noted below. If you want to meet for two hours, follow the times given in the right-hand column:

Section	90 Minutes	120 Minutes
CONNECT (discuss one or more of the opening questions for the session)	15 minutes	20 minutes
WATCH (watch the teaching material together and take notes)	20 minutes	20 minutes
DISCUSS (discuss the study questions you selected ahead of time)	35 minutes	50 minutes
RESPOND (write down key takeaways)	10 minutes	15 minutes
PRAY (pray together and dismiss)	10 minutes	15 minutes

As the group leader, it is up to you to keep track of the time and keep things on schedule. You might want to set a timer for each segment so both you and the group members know when your time is up. Don't be concerned if the group members are quiet or slow to share. People are often quiet when they are pulling together their ideas, and this might be a new experience for them. Just ask a question and let it hang in the air until someone shares. You can then say, "Thank you. What about others? What came to you when you watched that portion of the teaching?"

Group Dynamics

Leading a group through *The God of the Other Side* will prove to be highly rewarding both to you and your group members. But you still may encounter challenges along the way! Discussions can get off track. Group members may not be sensitive to the needs and ideas of others. Some might worry they will be expected to talk about matters that make them feel awkward. Others may express comments that result in disagreements. To help ease this strain on you and the group, consider the following ground rules:

- When someone raises a question or comment that is off the main topic, suggest that you deal with it another time, or, if you feel led to go in that direction, let the group know you will be spending some time discussing it.

- If someone asks a question that you don't know how to answer, admit it and move on. At your discretion, feel free to invite group members to comment on questions that call for personal experience.

- If you find one or two people are dominating the discussion time, direct a few questions to others in the group. Outside the main group time, ask the more dominating members to help you draw out the quieter ones. Work to make them a part of the solution instead of part of the problem.

- When a disagreement occurs, encourage the group members to process the matter in love. Encourage those on opposite sides to restate what they heard the other side say about the matter, and then invite each side to evaluate if that perception is accurate. Lead the group in examining other scriptures related to the topic and look for common ground.

When any of these issues arise, encourage your group members to follow these words from Scripture: "Love one another" (John 13:34), "If it is possible, as far as it depends on you, live at peace with everyone" (Romans 12:18), and "Be quick to listen, slow to speak and slow to become angry" (James 1:19). This will make your group time more rewarding and beneficial for everyone who attends.

Thank you again for taking the time to lead your group. You are making a difference in your group members' lives and having an impact on their journey toward a better understanding of the God of the Other Side.

Endnotes

1. "What Is the Significance of Decapolis in the Bible?" Got Questions, https://www.gotquestions.org/Decapolis-in-the-Bible.html.
2. "A Far Country: Decapolis," That the World May Know, https://www.thattheworldmayknow.com/a-far-country-decapolis.
3. Kathie Lee Gifford and Rabbi Jason Sobel, *The God of the Way* (Nashville, TN: W Publishing), 172.
4. "Roman Legion," Wikipedia, https://en.wikipedia.org/wiki/Roman_legion.
5. "The Roman Legion," University of Chicago, https://penelope.uchicago.edu/~grout/encyclopaedia_romana/britannia/wales/legio.html#:~:text=The%20Roman%20legion%20was%20a,of%20whom%20were%20Roman%20citizens.
6. Richard N. Longenecker, *The Expositor's Bible Commentary: Acts, The Expositor's Bible Commentary: Luke–Acts* (Grand Rapids, MI: Zondervan, 2007), 871.
7. "The Roman Legion," University of Chicago, https://penelope.uchicago.edu/~grout/encyclopaedia_romana/britannia/wales/legio.html#:~:text=The%20Roman%20legion%20was%20a,of%20whom%20were%20Roman%20citizens.
8. Walter W. Wessel and Mark L. Strauss, *The Expositor's Bible Commentary: Mark* (Grand Rapids, MI: Zondervan, 2007), 769.
9. "Sea of Galilee Boat," Wikipedia, https://en.wikipedia.org/wiki/Sea_of_Galilee_Boat.
10. J. I Packer, Merrill C. Tenney, and William White, Jr., *Public Life in Bible Times* (Nashville, TN: Thomas Nelson, 1985), 50–51.
11. Craig S. Keener, *The IVP Bible Background Commentary: New Testament* (Downers Grove, IL: InterVarsity Press, 1993), 68.
12. Richard Beck, *Unclean: Meditations on Purity, Hospitality, and Mortality* (Eugene, OR: Cascade Books, 2011).
13. Anthony Arthur, "Upton Sinclair," *The New York Times,* 2006, https://archive.nytimes.com/www.nytimes.com/ref/timestopics/topics_uptonsinclair.html.
14. "Samaria," Encyclopedia Brittanica, https://www.britannica.com/place/Samaria-historical-region-Palestine.
15. "What Is the Importance of Samaria in the Bible?" Got Questions, https://www.gotquestions.org/Samaria-in-the-Bible.html.
16. "Samaria," Encyclopedia Brittanica, https://www.britannica.com/place/Samaria-historical-region-Palestine.
17. Wayne A Brindle, "The Origin and History of the Samaritans," *Grace Theological Journal*, 5.1 (1984), chrome-extension://efaidnbmnnnibpcajpcglclefindmkaj/https://digitalcommons.liberty.edu/cgi/viewcontent.cgi?article=1071&context=sor_fac_pubs.
18. Wesley L. Gerig, "Water," Baker's Evangelical Dictionary of Biblical Theology, https://www.biblestudytools.com/dictionary/water/.
19. Shannon Jacobs, "The Wonderful Gift of Water and What It Symbolizes," Bible Keeper, December 7, 2022, https://www.biblekeeper.com/meaning-of-water-in-the-bible/.
20. "Hatfields and McCoys," Britannica, https://www.britannica.com/topic/Hatfields-and-McCoys.
21. Alyssa Roat, "The Samaritans: Hope from the History of a Hated People," Bible Study Tools, https://www.bible-studytools.com/bible-study/topical-studies/the-samaritans-hope-from-the-history-of-a-hated-people.html.
22. John MacArthur, "The Woman at the Well: A Strange Encounter on Sacred Ground," Grace to You, https://www.gty.org/library/blog/B210913/a-strange-encounter-on-sacred-ground.
23. "Hydration," MaineDOT Healthy Workforce, June 2020, https://www.maine.gov/mdot/challengeme/topics/2020/06Jun/#:~:text=Water%20carries%20nutrients%20and%20oxygen,protects%20and%20cushions%20vital%20organs.
24. Susan Nelson, "The Fascinating Symbolism of Water in the Bible: Nine Attributes," Woman of Noble Character, https://www.womanofnoblecharacter.com/water-in-the-bible/.
25. Henri Daniel-Rops, *Daily Life in the Time of Jesus* (Ann Arbor, MI: Servant Books, 1980), 115–116, 126.
26. Packer, Tenney, and White, *Public Life in Bible Times*, 2–4, 6.
27. Kathie Lee Gifford and Rabbi Jason Sobel, *The God of the Way* (Nashville, TN: W Publishing Group, 2022), 191.
28. Gifford and Sobel, *The God of the Way*, 215–216.
29. *Merriam-Webster's Dictionary*, s.v. "prodigal," https://www.merriam-webster.com/dictionary/prodigal.
30. John F. Thornton and Susan B. Varenne, eds., *Late Have I Loved Thee: Selected Writings of Saint Augustine on Love* (New York: Knopf Doubleday Publishing Group, 2006), xxxv.

31. "Caesarea's History," Caesarea Development Corporation, https://caesarea.com/en/rec-leisure/%D7%A1%D7%99%D7%A4%D7%95%D7%A8-%D7%94%D7%94%D7%99%D7%A1%D7%98%D7%95%D7%A8%D7%99%D7%94/#:~:text=-Caesarea's%20was%20first%20established%20as,absorbed%20into%20the%20Hasmonean%20Kingdom.

32. Longenecker, *The Expositor's Bible Commentary: Acts*, 942.

33. Longenecker, *The Expositor's Bible Commentary: Acts*, 947.

34. "Joppa (Jaffa)," Bible Places, https://www.bibleplaces.com/joppa/.

35. Rops, *Daily Life in the Time of Jesus*, 218–219.

36. "Inside First Century Home," That the World May Know, https://www.thattheworldmayknow.com/inside-first-century-home.

37. Verlyn D. Verbrugge, *The Expositor's Bible Commentary: 1 Corinthians* (Grand Rapids, MI: Zondervan, 2008), 265–266.

38. William W. Klein, *The Expositor's Bible Commentary: Ephesians* (Grand Rapids, MI: Zondervan, 2006), 105–107.

39. Robert K. Rapa, *The Expositor's Bible Commentary: Galatians* (Grand Rapids, MI: Zondervan, 2008), 601–603.

40. Luke J. Spencer, "The Ruin and Revival of the City that Built America," Messy Nessy, February 10, 2023, https://www.messynessychic.com/2023/02/08/the-ruin-and-revival-of-the-city-that-built-america/.

41. *Merriam-Webster's Dictionary*, s.v. "unity," https://www.merriam-webster.com/dictionary/unity?utm_campaign=sd&utm_medium=serp&utm_source=jsonld.

42. John Walton, Victor Matthews, and Mark Chavalas, *The IVP Bible Background Commentary: Old Testament* (Downers Grove, IL: IVP Academic, 2000), 556.

43. Walton et al., *The IVP Bible Background Commentary: Old Testament*.

44. *Blue Letter Bible*, s.v. "ek," https://www.blueletterbible.org/lexicon/g1537/KJV/tr/0-1/' s.v. "*kaleo*," https://www.blueletterbible.org/lexicon/g2564/KJV/tr/0-1/.

ALSO AVAILABLE

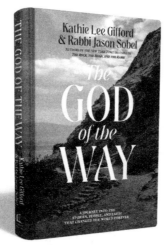

The God the Way
ISBN 9780785290438
On sale September 2022

The God of His Word
ISBN 9780310156673
On sale December 2022

The God of the How and When
ISBN 9780310156543
On sale November 2022

The God Who Sees
ISBN 9780310156802
On sale July 2023

The God of the Other Side
ISBN 9780310156932
On sale January 2024

Available wherever books are sold

W PUBLISHING GROUP

Harper*Christian* Resources

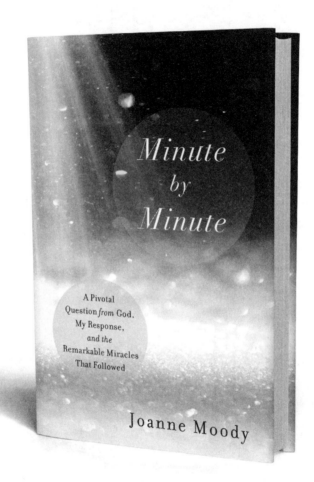

Video Study for Your Church or Small Group

In this six-session study, Kathie Lee Gifford helps you apply the principles in *The Rock, the Road, and the Rabbi* to your life. The study guide includes video notes, group discussion questions, and personal study and reflection materials for in-between sessions.

Study Guide
9780310147176

DVD
9780310095033

Available now at your favorite bookstore,
or streaming video on StudyGateway.com.